CONSCIENCE IN THE
NEW TESTAMENT

STUDIES IN BIBLICAL THEOLOGY

CONSCIENCE IN THE NEW TESTAMENT

A study of *Syneidesis* in the New Testament; in the
light of its sources, and with particular reference to
St. Paul: with some observations regarding its
pastoral relevance today

C. A. PIERCE
O.B.E., M.A., B.D. (Cantab.)
*Chaplain of Magdalene College
Cambridge*

SCM PRESS LTD
56 BLOOMSBURY STREET
LONDON

First published 1955

*Printed in Great Britain by
Robert Cunningham and Sons Ltd.,
Longbank Works, Alva*

'Dreadful consequences are derivable to Society caused by a plausible word wrested from its proper sense.'

C. DAUBENY: Guide to the Church

'It is necessary to know what conscience properly is, for of the number that make use of the word nineteen in twenty perhaps may be ignorant of its true meaning.'

ibid.

'Es ist überhaupt kein philosophischer Begriff gewesen, sondern er gehörte zu der grossen, noch allzu wenig erforschten Gruppe sittlicher Begriffe, die die philosophische Ethik als das ihr durch die Volkspsyche gebotene Material übernahm.'

NORDEN: Agnostos Theos

'This watchful auxiliary of the soul may be lulled to sleep but it can never die; it may be deadened but can never perish utterly. Happy is the man in whom it never sleeps. If it pain him the pain is for his good: it is as a thorn to guard him from the briers of iniquity: if he disregard it sad indeed be the after pangs and numberless the sore bruises. Let him but commit a crime: the little tell-tale conscience wakes and all happiness is gone.'

MICKLE: Conscience – a Tale of Life

CONTENTS

PREFACE

THE argument of this essay is brought to its conclusion in Chapter Twelve, so that the last two chapters are by way of Epilogue. Of what appears in them little could properly be said until after all the evidence had been adduced, examined and argued from; it would be out of place in a preface which, although written from outside and after the completion of the book, is printed at its beginning.

While, then, I have nothing to add here to what I have written in the main body, this is the best place to draw attention to those other works on this subject of which I am aware, but to which reference is nowhere made in the text or notes. For various reasons, among them lack of adequate library facilities until three years ago, these did not come into my hands until a relatively late stage in this study. The extent of my indebtedness to them will be obvious to the reader, as well as the reasons why, in spite of their existence, I have thought it worth while to continue writing this book.

In 1883 Paul Ewald produced a monograph *De vocis συνειδήσεως apud scriptores Novi Testamenti vi ac potestate commentatio*, in some ways answering the New Testament elements of Martin Kähler's much larger and more comprehensive study *Das Gewissen: die Entwickelung seiner Namen und seines Begriffes* which had appeared in 1878. The subject is touched on by Adolf Bonhöffer in his *Epiktet und das Neue Testament*, to which I have referred in the text, and which appeared in 1911: I mention this work again here as it is consciously opposed by Hans Böhlig in the relevant parts of his *Die Geisteskultur von Tarsos im augusteischen Zeitalter mit Berücksichtigung der paulinischen Schriften* which was published two years later. Böhlig claims the support of a paper by Steinmann, *Das Gewissen bei Paulus (Biblische Zeit- und Streitfragen, 1911)* which I have not been able to trace.

While I have tried to acknowledge all particular borrowings in the notes, my personal debts are far too many for detailed

9

enumeration. Chief among them, however, must always be that to my first teacher, the late Dr W. L. Knox, who taught me so much more than Theology. To the present Bishop of Durham, then Professor A. M. Ramsey, I am deeply indebted for his patience in discussing this work when it was only projected, as well as for his liberal encouragement in writing it. I must also acknowledge gratefully how much I learnt from him and from my fellow-members of the New Testament Seminar which he conducted while Regius Professor of Divinity at Cambridge. Dr Hans Kässmann gave generously of his time and invaluable help with the work of German scholars, and the criticisms of the Rev. W. H. Blyth-Martin at an early stage revealed a serious gap in the structure of this essay.

My thanks are also due to Mrs M. Wolff for her valuable help in preparing the original manuscript for typing, and to Miss E. Sutherland and her staff at the University Typewriting Office, whose long experience was so generously at my disposal for so much more than the mere direction of the typing.

In its original form this essay was approved in typescript by the University of Cambridge as a qualification for the degree of Bachelor of Divinity. In reducing it to a length and a form suitable for publication I was guided with patient wisdom by the Rev. R. Gregor Smith. My great thanks are also due to Miss M. Webb for preparing the two difficult typescripts with such care and despatch.

Magdalene College Cambridge   C. A. PIERCE
2nd August 1954

LIST OF ABBREVIATIONS

Papyrological and Epigraphical
Publications referred to in the Text and the
Analytical Index of Greek Sources

I. PAPYRI

Arch. Pap.:	*Archiv für Papyrusforschung.*
B.G.U.:	'Berliner Griechische Urkunden [Ägyptische Urkunden aus den Königlichen Museen zu Berlin.]' (Berlin 1895.)
Chrest.:	'Grundzüge und Chrestomathie der Papyruskunde.' (Leipzig and Berlin 1912.)
Flor:	'Papiri Fiorentini, documenti pubblici e privati dell' eta Romana e Bizantina.' Vol. III. Ed. G. Vitelli. (1915.)
Oxy.:	'The Oxyrhynchus Papyri,' Ed. Grenfell and Hunt. (London 1898.)
Par.:	'Notices et extraits des Papyrus Grecs du Musée du Louvre et de la Bibliothéque Nationale.' (Paris 1865.)
Reinach.:	'Papyrus Grecs et démotiques.' Ed. Th. Reinach. (Paris 1905.)
Ryl.:	'Catalogue of the Greek Papyri in the John Rylands Library at Manchester.' Vol. II. Ed. Hunt, Johnson & Martin. (1915.)

II. INSCRIPTIONS

Ath. Mitt.:	'Mitteilungen des Deutschen Archaeologischen Instituts – Athenische Abteilung.'
C.I.G.:	'Corpus Inscriptionum Graecarum.'
O.G.I.S.:	'Orientis Graeci Inscriptiones Selectae.' Ed. Dittenberger. (Leipzig 1903-5.)

Supp. Epigr.:   'Supplementum Epigraphicum Graecum.' Ed. Hondius – Leyden.

Syll.:   'Sylloge Inscriptionum Graecarum.' Ed. Dittenberger. (Leipzig 1888-1901.)

I

THE FALLACY OF
STOIC ORIGIN

THE quest for the meaning of *conscience* in the New Testament differs from most similar quests in that the word συνείδησις of which it is in the English versions a translation makes virtually no appearance in the Septuagint. This means that no recourse can be had, through this translation, to any Hebrew idea in the Old Testament from which material might be forthcoming for an elucidation of its meaning for the N.T. writers, and for St. Paul in particular.

Unless they invented it themselves to describe an experience peculiar to Christianity,[1] these writers must then have adopted the word and the idea connoted by it not from the Hebraic world of ideas but from the Hellenistic. Accordingly our search must begin with the surviving literary remains of that world.

The weight of authority leads us first to consider Stoicism. Such writers as Sanday and Headlam,[2] cautiously; Denney,[3] Dodd,[4] Moffatt[5] and Knowling,[6] all assert in one way or another that συνείδησις is a stoic term. The Stoics 'invented it'[7]; 'made much use of it'[8]; or 'first gave it philosophical importance'.[9]

But we soon discover that such an assertion is, firstly, hardly supported by the available evidence; secondly, inherently improbable; and thirdly, quite unnecessary.

For it only three quotations, at best, from Stoic writers can be offered in evidence: of these the most vital, as it was attributed to Epictetus, is of only doubtful origin.[10] Even were Epictetus

---

[1] As they did virtually with ἀγάπη.　[2] On Rom. 2.15 in *I.C.C.*
[3] *Ibid.* in *Expositors' Greek Testament*.　[4] *Ibid.* in *Moffatt Commentary*.
[5] On I Cor. 8.7 ff in *Moffatt Commentary*.
[6] On Acts 23.1 in *Expositors' Greek Testament*.
[7] Dodd, *loc. cit.*　[8] Denney, *loc. cit.*　[9] Knowling: Sanday and Headlam, *loc. cit.*
[10] Fr. 97 (Schweighaüser). It appears in Antonius' *Melissa*, and is attributed to Epictetus by Meibomius. This is the sole occasion in any work attributed to

the author beyond all possible doubt, it must still be remembered
that he was about four years old at the time of St. Paul's death.
If either influenced the other, it can only be the earlier who
influenced the later. In any case, further, the fragment would
still be a 'sport', having no proper place in the Epictetean corpus,
or, as will be seen, in Stoic writing in general. For if it be argued
that the remains of Epictetus are fragmentary, and that the argument from silence is thus weaker than usual, an earlier, more
'orthodox' Stoic provides the best answer. Chrysippus[1] predicates
συνείδησις of every living creature – not exclusively of man – and
means by it, as might be expected in a philosopher,[2] simply the
awareness or consciousness which a creature has of its own
composition. No moral element whatever is implied.

Such a moral element is however present in the third and last
item of evidence that can be offered in support of the assertion
of a Stoic origin for the Pauline συνείδησις. Marcus Aurelius[3]
closes a long list of virtues, and an exhortation to men to aspire
to them, with the words: 'that thy last hour coming upon thee
may find thee clear of conscience.' συνείδησις itself is not used
here, nor does the passage hint at any definition of the derivative
epithet which replaces it. The word here, therefore, has no technical significance for the author.[4] In any case the lateness of his
date makes him a poor witness.

That such meagre evidence is insufficient is obvious. But this
is hardly surprising, for it is inherently improbable that the
Pauline use of συνείδησις should derive from Stoicism. It will
be seen that in itself and in St. Paul's use of it the word includes
an emotional element: but for the Stoics emotions were, 'under
all circumstances, faults; and were an emotion to be useful, virtue
would be advanced by means of what is wrong'.[5] Despite this,

Epictetus in which such an expression, or the word συνείδησις, occurs. Its attribution to Epictetus rests on the slenderest authority. It is not consistent with the
picture of his thought that might otherwise be gained from his surviving works. On
such grounds as well as on those of style its Epictetean origin is considered most
doubtful by modern scholars [cf. Moulton and Milligan, *ad loc.*]. It is cited below,
p. 51, as Ex 54 and 84.
  [1] Cited by Diogenes Laertius vii.85 (Ex 65): φησὶν ὁ Χρύσιππος ἐν τῷ πρώτῳ περὶ
τελῶν, πρῶτον οἰκεῖον λέγων εἶναι παντὶ ζῴῳ τὴν αὑτοῦ σύστασιν καὶ τὴν ταύτης συνείδησιν.
  [2] See below, pp. 21 f.
  [3] 6.30. ἵν' οὕτως εὐσυνειδήτῳ σοι ἐπιστῇ ἡ τελευταία ὥρα.
  [4] See below, p. 49, n. 1.
  [5] Zeller: *Stoics, Epicureans and Sceptics*, p. 237.

however, it might still be held that the idea connoted by συνείδησις is in fact to be found employed by Stoics. They stressed, it is true, the necessity of the avoidance of emotion. But the idea connoted by συνείδησις, as we shall see, while not without at least an element of emotion, is of something very much to be avoided. The Stoics then, it could be argued, could have used the word to denote the emotion to be avoided in the moral sphere. We are not now concerned to refute such an argument: what is clear is that even if they did use such an idea, συνείδησις was not the word selected to connote it. Epictetus talks of a κοινὸς νοῦς which he defines formally in the words: 'There are some things which all men who are not utterly perverse recognise by their common faculties'[1]: by the whole context he shows how little importance he attaches to it, and in any case the definition shows that such an idea is far from resembling that which this study will show συνείδησις to connote. The same can be said of what must be the same notion, expressed in such different terms as συναίσθησις, or παρακολούθησις (τῶν φαντασιῶν) or, with particular reference to the sense of decency, τὸ ἐντρεπτικόν which Epictetus employs, and τὸ αἰδῆμον which Marcus Aurelius uses as well as he. It can thus be stated summarily that while it is doubtful whether the idea connoted by συνείδησις is used, let alone originated, by Stoicism, it is quite certain that συνείδησις itself is not.

Such a judgment of course emphatically rejects the attribution to Epictetus of the *Melissa* fragment[2]: but the reasons given for so doing are reinforced by the facts given above.

The assumption then of a Stoic origin for the Pauline συνείδησις rests on quite insufficient evidence, and is inherently improbable. Forced thus to widen the field of our search, we find this assumption to have been, furthermore, entirely unnecessary. The pseudo-Epictetus fragment has already offered a hint. The use of τῷ ἰδίῳ συνειδότι in the final sentence, in parallel with τῇ ἐμφύτῳ συνειδήσει in the second, makes it clear that τὸ συνειδός is, here at least, interchangeable with συνείδησις. This clue leads straight

---

[1] III.6.8: ἐστί τινα ἅ οἱ μὴ παντάπασιν διεστραμμένοι τῶν ἀνθρώπων κατὰ τὰς κοινὰς ἀφορμὰς ὁρῶσιν.
[2] Epictetus: Fr. 97 (Schweighaüser), cited on p. 51 as Ex 54 and 84. Cf. p. 13, n. 10; also Bonhöffer: *Epiktet u.d. N.T.*, p. 156, to which is owed the reference given above.

to Stobaeus' chapter: Περὶ τοῦ Συνειδότος.[1] This – as the title of
the book promises – comprises a catena of apophthegms culled
from a wide variety of authors to illustrate this subject. There
are sixteen apophthegms in all; as relevant to τὸ συνειδός this
excerptor of the sixth century A.D. includes quotations which
employ αὐτῷ συνειδέναι τι; αὐτῷ συνιστορεῖν τι; σύνεσις and
συνείδησις, as well as τὸ συνειδός. It is quite plain, therefore, that
συνείδησις is but one of a group of cognate or similar words or
phrases that may be used interchangeably to express exactly the
same idea.

It is accordingly from a study of the use of these words and
phrases over thirteen centuries of Greek literature that we may
hope to discover with reasonable precision the meaning that
συνείδησις had when St. Paul, as we shall show later,[2] introduced
it into Christianity, complete with its connotation. At present it
suffices to notice that he is the first N.T. writer to use it: that he
does so more often than any other Biblical writer; and that he
builds most upon it. Accordingly his use of it may be taken as
the norm for Christianity. He, however, no more than other N.T.
writers, wrote for professional philosophers. It is therefore in
general at the level, not of technical philosophy, but of the
commonplaces of everyday colloquial usage that his meaning
must be sought. Such usage it is true always adopts, with understanding more or less confused, jargon fashionable among the
professionals in philosophy, as well as in other fields – even if at
times it lags behind the professionals and picks up a jargon
already going out of fashion. There is thus always an element of
'popular philosophy' in popular speech: and this is no less true
of Hellenistic *koinē* at the beginning of the Christian era. This
accounts for the apparently philosophic element in St. Paul's
proclamation, of the facts of the revelation in Christ, in terms of
popular commonplace, as such scholars as W. L. Knox and A. D.
Nock have sufficiently shown. But the assumption of a Stoic
origin for the idea of *the conscience* having been abandoned, it is
plain that St. Paul's starting point must be sought in some popular
idea current at the time when he was writing.

The group of words and phrases, then, of which συνείδησις
is but one, is found again and again, throughout the range of

[1] III.xxiv.   [2] See pp. 63 ff.

Greek writing as a whole – not in literature only – from the sixth century B.C. to the seventh century A.D. It is used by every possible sort of writer: by philosophers and poets; by tragic and comic playwrights – and who more in touch with popular usage than the comedian; by historians and novelists; by engineers and physicians; by orators and rhetoricians; by learned critics and simple commissioners of domestic inscriptions: by writers of private correspondence. It is in fact an 'everyday' group of words expressing a commonplace idea – truly popular, and belonging rather to 'folk-wisdom' than to 'popular philosophy' – or, rather, second-hand philosophical jargon. In commenting on its first appearance in Greek literature,[1] Norden[2] rightly observes that here there enters a conception that was not of Democritus' own creating. 'It is not a philosophical conception at all', he says, 'but belongs to the great and still too little investigated group of ethical conceptions, which were taken up by Ethics as material, but originated in popular thought.[3] So it might be expressed at the present day – but in the language of antiquity it would be: "The Seven Sages have thought it so".'

At the end of this book may be found an analytical index of a large selection of examples of the use of this group of words and phrases. Many of them will be found referred to again in the text, and some, the normative or the more illuminating, will have to be examined more closely. It is significant that no substantial change is observable in the idea conveyed by this group throughout its long history, even after the establishment of the ecumenical influence of Christianity. Stobaeus compiled his catena in the sixth century A.D. and included, with no sense of inconsistency, apophthegms from the sixth, fifth and fourth centuries B.C., and the first century A.D. It is, therefore, safe to say that whatever we find to be the content of the idea, this was St. Paul's starting-point in his use of συνείδησις. It may be possible further to deduce that any adjustments which he made to the idea to fit it into his general scheme, and any development of it that he introduced, were not of such significance as to make the word

[1] Democritus: Fr. 297 (Diels), cited p. 34, n. 1 below, as Ex 72.
[2] *Agnostos Theos*, p. 136 n. Norden in taking this fragment as the earliest evidence available presumably discounts the ascription of the use of the word to Periander and Bias by Stobaeus, to whose chapter he refers. Cf. also p. 37 below.
[3] *Volkspsyche*.

17

unrecognisable by his pagan contemporaries and their successors.

The word, from which all the words and phrases in this group spring, is σύνοιδα. This occurs once in the N.T.[1] but there is some ground for supposing that Luke or his source, in the use of συνιδών[2] and συνιδόντες[3] intended this participle also to be understood as standing virtually for an aorist of σύνοιδα rather than of συνοράω–although the distinction is perhaps very fine. This very common word means basically, as its composition shows, *I know in common with*. Its most frequent general use is to indicate knowledge about another person as a potential witness for or against him. Reasonably there develops from this the sense of, simply, *I bear witness*.[4]

Other senses that arise are: (*a*) that of being privy with another –a shared secret. This leads to: (*b*) in which the *guilty* secret is isolated–*guilty complicity*. It can also mean (*c*) simply, *awareness*, or *consciousness* and thence (*d*) *I know well*. None of these senses call for detailed study, nor for illustration, for there is no evidence to suggest that the absolute use of this word bears directly upon the idea under discussion.

The colloquial phrase, however: ὡς ἂν συνειδῇς,[5] meaning *please yourself* or *it's up to you* leads us directly, by way of the absolute usage, to a particular construction of this word which is far commoner than any other use of it–the construction αὐτῷ συνειδέναι. It is an understanding of this phrase, although it appears but once in the N.T.,[6] which we shall find to be of the greatest value for our enquiry. In itself this phrase suggests a variety of ideas–which might appear singly or in combination: *to share knowledge with one's self–to be privy . . . with one's self–to hug a (possibly guilty) secret to one's self–to be a witness for or against one's self* or *to bear witness to one's self.*[7]

---

[1] Acts 5.2. [2] Acts 12.12. [3] Acts 14.6.

[4] as in, e.g., Isocrates vii.50: σύνοιδα τοῖς πλείστοις αὐτῶν ἥκιστα χαίρουσι.

[5] Aetius xiii.2.

[6] I Cor. 4.4.

[7] For the present, indeed for every practical purpose, the phrase αὐτῷ συνιστορεῖν, may be treated as an alternative form of αὐτῷ συνειδέναι. In commenting on Menander (Fr. 632, Kock's numbering)–ὁ συνιστορῶν αὐτῷ τι–(Ex 34 and 57, see below, p. 25) Kock says: συνιστορῶν i.e. συνειδώς. It is the exigences of metre that compel the use of the alternative form here. ἴστωρ–the basic word underlying ἱστορέω–comes, as Liddell and Scott point out, 'no doubt from the root Ϝιδ- [εἴδω], for it has the Ϝ in Homer and is so written in Boeotian inscriptions.' If prosodic convenience requires an alternative to συνειδώς, this word, patently from the same root, suggests

Of the three substantival equivalents for the verbal phrase, one –τὸ συνειδός–whose relation to σύνοιδα is obvious enough, does not occur at all in the N.T.: the second, σύνεσις, occurs frequently in both LXX and N.T., but always in the ordinary sense of *understanding*.[1] Its use as a synonym for συνείδησις is in any case very rare. συνείδησις, on the other hand, while common enough in non-Biblical Greek, has the field virtually to itself in the N.T. It will be shown: (*a*) that it is simply an alternative for τὸ συνειδός (and for σύνεσις in its occasional use) and (*b*) that these three words are substantival equivalents for σύνοιδα, but most particularly for ἐμαυτῷ σύνοιδα.[2] If there be any significant difference between τὸ συνειδός and συνείδησις it appears to be that the latter is wider in its scope than the former, being capable of standing for any sense of σύνοιδα besides its main usage as representing ἐμαυτῷ σύνοιδα: while τὸ συνειδός is far more rigorously, although not quite entirely, confined to representing ἐμαυτῷ σύνοιδα only.

If it is of importance to ask why the N.T. prefers συνείδησις to the other words or phrases in the group, this question divides itself into two halves. The preference of a noun to a verbal phrase, particularly if the construction of that phrase be somewhat complex, is a mark of the popular development of language. The reason for the preference of συνείδησις to σύνεσις is simply that the former is less ambiguous: the latter can only be seen by its context to represent αὐτῷ συνειδέναι. If a substantive be required that can carry a plain meaning without any explanatory context, συνείδησις is the obvious choice.

There is little reason apparent in either the nature or the usage of τὸ συνειδός or of συνείδησις for preferring either to the other. But a possible explanation of the N.T.'s preference of the latter suggests itself immediately from an examination of the backgrounds of the authors who use them. The evidence is certainly not sufficient for proof, but the probability is none the less strong that the N.T. writers did not choose συνείδησις for some reasons of their own but found it ready chosen. The writers who use συνείδησις are predominantly Asiatic in origin, while those who

itself inevitably, although it is a rare word in any case and is not elsewhere so employed.

[1] If it has any special nuance it is that of *understanding in detail* as contrasted with σοφία–*Understanding in general principle*.

[2] Below, pp. 30 ff.

prefer τὸ συνειδός are predominantly European[1]: writers are of course less local in their usage than those who use language only for speech, but their casual expressions may sometimes give them away. There may be here then sufficient indication that in the 'dialect' of the environment in which the N.T. was written συνείδησις was already the established preference.

[1] This assertion may be verified by reference to the analytical index of Greek Sources.

II

THE BACKGROUND OF συνείδησις

By analysis[1] of the use of these words and phrases it is possible to distinguish two main categories. In the case of αὐτῷ συνειδέναι these are simply: (a) a use in a non-moral context, confined to philosophers in technical or semi-technical writings–best paraphrased as *I am conscious within my self that . . .* or *I am conscious of . . . within my self*: and (b) a use developing from (a) wherein the content of the consciousness is the moral quality of the subject's own acts or behaviour.

In (a) the object of συνειδέναι or the activity of its subject,[2] although doubtless desirable or undesirable in the author's eyes, is not so in terms of ethics.

Thus Alcibiades, in his encomium of Socrates[3] declares that he is even now aware within himself that were he to listen to the philosopher he would have no power to resist but would succumb to the same emotions as of old. Although the emotions to which he refers are remorseful, and therefore moral in reference, here it is only of his helplessness to resist the Socratic homily of which he takes knowledge within himself–is conscious.

The obviously significant thing about this category is that all the examples of it are from Plato or Aristotle, nor can any example of the latter's usage be placed in any other.[4] Plato, however, also uses the phrase in ways that demand classification in

---

[1] The reader is referred from henceforward to the data supplied in the analytical index at the end of this book. Examples of usages cited are cross-referenced to a serial number in this index, the abbreviation *Ex* followed by this number being attached to every reference given.

[2] Column V in the analytical index; and see below, p. 32 f, for the various constructions in which this phrase is employed.

[3] Plato: *Symp.* 216ᵃ (Ex 4): καὶ ἔτι γε νῦν σύνοιδ᾽ ἐμαυτῷ ὅτι εἰ ἐθέλοιμι παρέχειν τὰ ὦτα, οὐκ ἂν καρτερήσαιμι, ἀλλὰ ταὐτὰ ἂν πάσχοιμι. The use of a ὅτι clause to express the object of αὐτῷ συνειδέναι is very rare. It does, however, occur once in the N.T. also (II Cor. 1.12), q.v., p. 87.

[4] Although in Arist: *Hist. An.* 618ᵃ.26 (Ex 5) δειλίαν is the object of αὐτῷ συνειδέναι –a word possibly descriptive of a moral condition–the subject is *the cuckoo*. In any

category (*b*)[1]; but he, although a professional philosopher, wrote also for a wider, if still cultured, public, while Aristotle's remains are lecture notes and severely technical; no popular audience was in mind. We may thus classify this usage as a philosopher's technical term, and notice its lack of any interest in the ethical quality of the object of consciousness. For convenient reference this classification will be abbreviated to PTI [Philosophic–Technical–Indifferent (ethically)].

PTI usage then of αὐτῷ συνειδέναι is that which is best rendered in English as *I am conscious of . . . in myself* or *I feel that I . . .* It is confined to two authors and both of them are professional philosophers.[2]

It will soon become clear that the predominant use of this phrase and its dependents is neither philosophic[3] nor technical, while the N.T. usage is emphatically popular.[4] As, further, our present concern is with the place of συνείδησις in ethics, it is plain that PTI is, apart from such notice and classification, beyond the scope of this enquiry. It is to the second main category that our attention must be devoted.

In this category the content of consciousness[5] is the moral quality of the subject's own acts or character.

As the object of our enquiry is to *discover* the connotation, in a moral context, of the group of words to which συνείδησις belongs, it is plain that at this early stage any idiomatic translation of these words would be question-begging. Where examples are cited in translation, therefore, αὐτῷ συνειδέναι will henceforward be rendered quite literally *to know with one's self*, and the nouns will be left untranslated.

---

case Aristotle later explains his use of the phrase as meaning *consciousness of its inability to fend for its young*, i.e. *of helplessness*. A close parallel is thus afforded with the Platonic example above.

[1] Plato: *Apol.* 21[b], *Phaedr.* 235[c], *Symp.* 216[a] and [b], *Rep.* 331[a] and 607[c] (Ex 1, 2, 4, 11, 25 and 26), when examined together, and in the order of their appearance in the index, are seen to span in easy gradation most of the possible uses of the phrase, from the technical to the popular, via the literary, as they will be defined in this chapter, by reference to the content (Column V) and the result (Column VIII) of αὐτῷ συνειδέναι.

[2] Chrysippus in the citation (Ex 65) above, p. 14, n. 1, uses the noun συνείδησις to represent the PTI αὐτῷ συνειδέναι. He too, of course, is a professional philosopher.

[3] Of the 89 examples set out in the analytical index only 6 can be classified PTI, 5 of which are uses of αὐτῷ συνειδέναι (Ex 1-5), and only one of συνείδησις (Ex 65). Cf. also Norden's comment on Democritus Fr. 297 (Ex 72) p. 17, above.

[4] Cf. also p. 16 f, above.   [5] I.e. Column V in the analytical index.

To the whole of this category the classification M (moral content) will be applied for reference. It demands, and is patient of,
further subdivision. Obviously the first two such sub-categories
within a moral context are *Good* and *Bad*. We shall call the latter
sub-category MB (moral–bad) and shall find it to consist yet
again of three classes of variant use. As the vast majority of the
examples adduced are MB,[1] this sub-category will engage our
attention most and is best taken last.

The *Good* sub-category we shall call MPG (moral–positively
good) for reference–*positively* good in order to differentiate it
from the negative form of MB.[2]

MPG usage of αὐτῷ συνειδέναι is most effectively illustrated by
Xenophon.[3] 'We know with ourselves', he writes, 'that we
began as children and still continue in the practice of noble and
good works.' The complexity of construction compels us to
render the object of knowledge as though it were expressed in
indirect speech.[4] Xenophon actually wrote 'we having begun . . .
being practitioners . . . know with ourselves.' συνειδέναι is thus
here used without an object, the content of knowledge being
conveyed by two participles agreeing with its subject. In any
case this content is one of good character, expressed in the most
positive terms. It is a grammatically legitimate enough usage, so
that its comparative rarity[5] is not easy to explain and is therefore
the more significant for this enquiry. For this is the only MPG
example of αὐτῷ συνειδέναι in which we can have complete confidence, and at best there are only two others.[6]

---

[1] Of the 89 examples referred to in the analytical index 12 are not M; of the
remaining 77 M examples at the least 67 are MB, and 4 more are only excluded from
that category very doubtfully, and in order to avoid all suspicion of tendenciousness.
Nor is this result in any way contrived. While the non-M examples have been
selected for purposes of illustration, no such selection has been brought to bear on
the M examples, and all that I have been able to find have been included.

[2] q.v. below, p. 25 ff.

[3] *Cyr.* I.v.11 (Ex 8): σύνισμεν ἡμῖν αὐτοῖς ἀπὸ παίδων ἀρξάμενοι ἀσκηταὶ ὄντες τῶν
καλῶν κἀγαθῶν ἔργων. The constructions in which the phrase is employed, and which
therefore underlie the nouns, being of great significance for an understanding of
the latter, will repay most careful attention. See below, p. 32.

[4] Cf. Plato: *Symp.* 216ᵃ (Ex 4), cited above, p. 21, n. 3.

[5] Cf. p. 47, n. 1, below.

[6] (a) Soph.: Fr. 669 (Dindorf): Ἦ δεινὸν ἄρ' ἦν, ἡνίκ' ἄν τις ἐσθλὸς ὢν / αὐτῷ συνειδῇ.
The Sophoclean fragment owes its preservation to Stobaeus (*op. cit.*) alone, and as it
stands without context it is barely comprehensible, as is evidenced by the misplaced
ingenuity of the many quite unjustifiable attempts at emendation which it has
stimulated (cf. Jebb, *ad loc*). Sophocles wrote at a stage in the development of the

The content of αὐτῷ συνειδέναι in the remaining examples of its use[1] is invariably bad–whether a disposition, a condition or an action. But knowledge with one's self of this badness entails consequences. Thus he who knows with himself that he has neglected oaths sworn before the gods, can never again be counted happy[2]; and these are the two marks of every example of the MB use–the bad act, the bad disposition from which it springs or the bad condition or character resulting from it[3]; and the unhappy consequences of knowing such an act, disposition or character with one's self.[4] In the normal use the badness is as here specifically expressed, and usually the consequence is also defined. We may call this normal (MBNorm for reference) firstly because it is the most frequent[5]; secondly, and far more cogently, because the other two uses of MB assume and depend upon it.

This is self evident in the case of that use in which the content of αὐτῷ συνειδέναι is not specifically expressed but its badness is shown, either by the context or by the consequence specified, to be taken for granted as implicit in the use of the phrase itself. There is some justification for supposing this to be the popular usage; for in literature this use of αὐτῷ συνειδέναι occurs only in

usage of the phrase so much earlier than the first discoverable literary traces of the popular usage, that we seem compelled to classify the fragment as MPG, and either to suppose that if we knew the context it would be plain why the self-knowledge of τις ἐσθλὸς ὤν should be δεινόν, or to interpret δεινόν in some such way as Jebb's just conceivable *a powerful aid*. Stobaeus, however, included it in his catena nearly 1000 years later: that he omitted any clue as to the context makes it all but certain that he interpreted it by the later popular and absolute form of MB (q.v. just below) as meaning 'it is a terrible thing for one who is (normally) virtuous to have something on his conscience.' This fragment accordingly appears twice in the analytical index: as Ex 7, MPG, interpreted as Sophoclean usage, and as Ex 35, MB–Absolute, interpreted as Stobaean.

(b) Dem: *Ep.* II.20. (Ex 6)–εἰς τὴν πατρίδα εὔνοιαν ἐμαυτῷ σύνοιδα–is a borderline case in that the phrase is here best rendered by *I feel*. In any case the opinion of most scholars that this epistle is not by Demosthenes is confirmed by the gulf between this use and that in the undisputedly Demosthenic writings (cf. *de Fals. Leg.* 208, cited below, p. 48, and 210, *de Corona* 263 (Ex 28-30)), which is consistently the popular MB as might be expected in a public speaker who knew pre-eminently how to persuade the public–and, obviously, therefore what words meant to that public.

[1] Twenty-seven examples out of a total of thirty-five.

[2] Xen: *Anab.* II.v.7 (Ex 21): ὅστις δὲ τούτων (*the oaths*) σύνοιδεν αὐτῷ παρημεληκὼς, τοῦτον ἐγὼ οὔποτ' ἂν εὐδαιμονίσαιμι. The tense of the participle (perf.) should be noticed. The construction is participial as in *Cyr.* I.v.11 (Ex 8), cited above, p. 23.

[3] Column V in the analytical index.

[4] Column VIII in the analytical index.

[5] Sixteen out of twenty-seven MB examples of αὐτῷ συνειδέναι are MBNorm.

Aristophanes and Menander. A fragment of the latter[1] declares that he who knows anything at all with himself, no matter how brave he is, will be reduced to the extreme of terror by this knowledge. From the writer's use of the most indefinite word possible as the object of knowledge, it is absolutely certain that he takes it for granted that anything whatever that may be a proper object of αὐτῷ συνειδέναι produces this result. In other words popular usage of αὐτῷ συνειδέναι in his day was so limited that he, or his public, could not conceive of anything which a man might συνειδέναι αὐτῷ that would not take from him all his courage. As in this category, then, αὐτῷ συνειδέναι is used absolutely to convey *by itself* the badness of its content–even when it is ironically described in terms ostensibly good, we may call this the absolute form of MB–MBA for reference.

The third subdivision of the MB use is the negative form, which will be referred to as MBNeg. In this the content of αὐτῷ συνειδέναι[2] is still bad, but, a negative being introduced into the construction, the consequence of such knowledge[3] is reversed, being no longer unhappy but happy indeed. As Xenophon has already illustrated for us MBNorm,[4] he may also provide us with an illustration of this usage. Cyrus is exhorted to the pursuit of virtue, for this will lead to joy in prayer and a sure and certain hope of favourable response to it, in that he may reckon that he has no knowledge with himself of ever having neglected this pursuit.[5] The ground of this assurance and joy is the absence of precisely that inward consciousness of neglect, which, in the former example,[4] precluded him that had it from ever being counted

---

[1] Men.: Fr. 632 (Kock), cited by Stobaeus (*op. cit.*)

ὁ συνιστορῶν αὑτῷ τι κἂν ᾖ θρασύτατος
ἡ σύνεσις αὐτὸν δειλότατον εἶναι ποιεῖ:

on συνιστορῶν see p. 18, n. 7. As this fragment uses σύνεσις as well as, and defined in terms of the verbal phrase, it appears twice in the analytical index; as Ex 34, of αὐτῷ συνειδέναι, and again as Ex 57, of σύνεσις. Cf. also Ar: *Eq.* 184 (Ex 33) cited below, p. 45, where the other comedian makes his point that in the topsy-turvy world of Athenian politics goodness has changed places with evil, by making καλόν τι the object of αὐτῷ συνειδέναι but predicating unhappy consequences. It is more than possible that he makes the equivalent point in relation to the Law Courts by the same method in *Vesp.* 999 (Ex 19); cf. also below, p. 45.

[2] Column V in the analytical index.

[3] Column VIII in the analytical index.

[4] Cf. Xen: *Anab.* II.v.7 (Ex 21), cited above, p. 24, n. 2.

[5] Xen: *Cyr.* I.vi.4 (Ex 10): διά γ' ἐκείνας τὰς ἐπιμελείας ἥδιον μὲν ἔρχῃ πρὸς τοὺς θεοὺς δεησόμενος, ἐλπίζεις δὲ μᾶλλον τεύξεσθαι ὧν ἂν δέῃ, ὅτι συνειδέναι σαυτῷ δοκεῖς οὐπώποτ' ἀμελήσας αὐτῶν.

25

happy. These two examples are illuminating in juxtaposition, in that it is the position of *never* alone that changes. In the first case the dictum might be summarised: 'Never neglect-happy': and in the second: 'Neglect–never happy.' In neither case, however, has the happiness or unhappiness any external cause: the presence or absence of the internal αὐτῷ συνειδέναι is the sole source of both.

From the comparison of these two examples it is luminously clear that, wherever the negative be placed in the construction expressing knowledge and its content, it is the *knowledge* that is negated; and αὐτῷ συνειδέναι thus being absent the normal consequence of its presence is reversed. This is no less true of every MBNeg occurrence, as is readily seen if the three forms of MB be reduced to their simplest terms. Thus MBA's ἐμαυτῷ τι σύνοιδα means always ἐμαυτῷ κακόν τι σύνοιδα[1] [MBNorm]. ἐμαυτῷ τι οὐ σύνοιδα is simply not Greek: the language automatically converts it to μηδὲν ἐμαυτῷ σύνοιδα[2]–but the former is none the less precisely what it means, even when it appears in the form μηδὲν κακὸν ἐμαυτῷ σύνοιδα. It is not consciousness of the absence of wrong, but absence of the consciousness of wrong that is so expressed. It is not a case of litotes.[3] While, therefore, MBNeg lies, and is placed in the analytical index, between MPG and MBNorm, it cannot be said to bridge the gap between them as it is strictly a variant form of the latter. It is in any case misleading to suppose that the negation of one content implies the affirmation of another. A bottle containing no whisky is not necessarily for that reason full of tea. It is more probably empty. So the αὐτῷ συνειδέναι whose content is, e.g. μηδὲν κακόν does not necessarily have ἀγαθόν as its content. In fact, that the emptiness of the bottle is defined as *no whisky* indicates that it is expected to contain whisky or nothing–that it is a whisky-bottle. Thus MBNeg entirely corroborates the conclusion already amply demonstrated by MBA, that MBNorm is in fact the normal use

---

[1] Cf. Men.: Fr. 632 (Kock) (Ex 34 and 57), cited above, p. 25 and note.

[2] μὴ is the negative in αὐτῷ συνειδέναι constructions because the participial construction is always implied: on these constructions see below, p. 32 f.

[3] Where litotes is intended οὐ is of course the negative; cf. Eur: *Med.* 495 (Ex 18): ἐπεὶ σύνοισθά γ' εἰς ἔμ' οὐκ εὔορκος ὤν. Euripides omits the reflexive pronoun for reasons of prosody only; he was also compelled to do so in *Or.* 395 f (Ex 17 and 56, q.v. below, p. 47, n. 5).

of this phrase–that the content of αὑτῷ συνειδέναι is bad unless definitely stated otherwise. That or nothing is its content. If then badness be the proper content of αὑτῷ συνειδέναι, the variety of words used to express it[1] is in some cases the result merely of the use of a synonym: and in others of a desire more closely to define the nature of the badness: and it is, further, hardly surprising that the consequences of its 'emptiness' should in the case of MBNeg[2] be described in such glowing terms. In the use of this phrase, then, a clear line of relationship is to be seen running through the examples set out analytically in the index. In PTI the content is (morally) indifferent: in MPG it is positively good. In MBNeg τὸ αὑτῷ συνειδέναι is 'empty'. In MBNorm the content is badness while in MBA it is bad but does not in the author's opinion need to be stated, as being sufficiently indicated by the use of αὑτῷ συνειδέναι.

Although MBA is only less rare than MPG the sources of the examples are such that there are good grounds for supposing this to be the popular usage: certainly Menander and Aristophanes expected their audiences to be able to understand it: while Stobaeus, as we saw,[3] was most probably himself misled into understanding it here where he should not have done so. If PTI be taken as belonging to another, and relatively remote, world and MPG as a rare literary use, MBNorm and MBNeg are the standard use–properly in touch with the popular.

It is not hard to see how the 'popular' use arises–even if it be not actually the source of the rather curious construction of the literary use. If a man say σύνοιδα ἐμαυτῷ δείν' εἰργασμένος[4] it is but the fuller alternative, as we shall see, to σύνοιδα ἐμαυτῷ δεινά. In the latter expression an implicit εἰργασμένος can always be understood, *mutatis mutandis*. Whichever form, full or elliptical, is used, therefore, it is possible to construe it as δείν' εἰργασμένος, ἐμαυτῷ σύνοιδα. ἐμαυτῷ σύνοιδα is thus taken as the–unpleasant–fact, and δείν' εἰργασμένος as

---

[1] Column V in the analytical index.
[2] In addition to Xen: *Cyr.* I.vi.4 (Ex 10), cited above, p. 25, and note, cf. Column VIII in the analysis of Plato: *Rep.* 331ᵃ (Ex 11); Isoc: *to Nicocles* 59 (Ex 13); Antiphanes ap Stobaeus, *loc. cit.* (Ex 14); Diogenes ap Stobaeus, *loc. cit* (Ex 15); and, in the case of συνείδησις, Column VII in the analysis of Herodian: *Hist.* VI.iii.4 (Ex 69), cited below, p. 36 and note.
[3] Cf. p. 23, n. 6 (*a*), above.
[4] Cf. Eur: *Or.* 395 f (Ex 17 and 56), cited below, p. 47 and note.

the antecedent[1] cause, which need not always be expressed.

These findings may thus be summed up: just as *Num?* expects the answer *No!*, so αὐτῷ συνειδέναι expects the content *bad*; unless, as is found very rarely, the opposite is explicitly stated.

---

[1] Cf. below, pp. 43 ff; it will be shown that it is beyond doubt a question of *antecedent* cause.

III

THE USE OF συνείδησις

THE accurate classification and the precise exegesis on the basis of which such a conclusion may be reached is of course much more possible of a complete and elaborate verbal phrase than of a noun. It will however not have been lost labour, but will prove to have been the indispensable preliminary to the attempt to discover the precise connotation of συνείδησις, if it can be shown that the equation τὸ αὑτῷ συνειδέναι = συνείδησις (and, although this is less important, τὸ συνειδός and, on occasion, σύνεσις also) is valid in every M context.

This is sufficient for our purpose as it is only the M use of συνείδησις that concerns us. Before making this demonstration, however, we must pause to notice that, while PTI is of course the only non-M category of αὑτῷ συνειδέναι,[1] yet, when we apply to the substantival expressions the system of classification derived from our analysis of the use of that phrase, we find that to the five categories already analysed a sixth must be added. For these five are classifications of the usage only of αὑτῷ συνειδέναι whereas τὸ συνειδός and συνείδησις can be used to represent substantivally not only this phrase, but also the simple συνειδέναι. When therefore they appear employed in the latter way, they must be classified NA [not applicable–that is, to the present enquiry].

Thus Demosthenes plucks consolation from the fact that, although, as he has systematically to answer charges of illegal activity, he will make no mention of the major part of his policy and administration, nevertheless each one of his hearers knows

---

[1] For a PTI use of συνείδησις cf. Chrysippus ap Diog. Laert. vii.85 (Ex 65) cited p. 14 and note, above. I am not aware that τὸ συνειδός was ever used in this way. If it were not self-evident from this passage there would of course be no difficulty in showing, were it relevant, that the equation is no less valid in the PTI context.

about this as well as he does.[1] τὸ συνειδός is used simply to represent τὸ συνειδέναι–the knowledge shared with the speaker by his audience. It is thus only relevant to our present purpose as an exception that makes trial of the rule that is becoming clear.

It is probable that no further proof is needed of the validity of our equation than the fact that Stobaeus[2] includes indifferently, in a chapter headed 'Concerning τὸ συνειδός', excerpts which employ not only this articular participle, but also the verbal phrase in both its forms, as well as συνείδησις and σύνεσις. The homogeneity of his chapter suggests that he was right to do so, and this suggestion is further borne out by the similar but more impressive–for a far larger number of excerpts is involved–homogeneity of the material presented in the analytical index to this book; and not least therein by the fact that all that material is so readily patient of the same system of classification.

In order however that in this vital matter there may be not the least doubt, a brief proof in detail is desirable. We have already met one substantive to which the meaning of the verbal phrase is held by the writer concerned to be in the context absolutely equivalent. Menander[3] replaces ὁ συνιστορῶν αὑτῷ τι in the first line of his couplet with ἡ σύνεσις in the second, because he wishes to make the subject of the former the object of the latter, while leaving it clear that what has upon him the unhappy effect concerned is in fact that same internal condition of which he is himself the subject. The noun in fact has got to mean τὸ αὑτῷ συνιστορεῖν τι if the required sense is to be conveyed at all. Euripides[4] does almost exactly the same thing when he makes Orestes say that he suffers σύνεσις in that he knows with himself that he has done terrible things. But this line is cited complete by Plutarch, who

---

[1] Dem: *de Corona* 110 (Ex 36): ὁμοίως παρ' ὑμῶν ἑκάστῳ τὸ συνειδὸς ὑπάρχειν μοι. Demosthenes was well aware of the idea that others express, as will be seen, by τὸ συνειδός: but in common with the rest of the writers of his day he expressed it by αὑτῷ συνειδέναι cf. later in this same speech (263–Ex 30); also references on p. 23, n. 6 (*b*), above. τὸ συνειδός in this sense is an early usage: later writers preferred συνείδησις; for which cf. Soranus i.4 (Ex 60): συνείδησις τῶν ἀλγημάτων (of childbirth) as making the best midwife; also *Pap.*: *Par.*p. 422.7 (Ex 62); *Pap.*:*Oxy.*I.123.13. (Ex 63), in which it is used of the deliberate imparting of information: and Hippocrates: *Ep.* I (Ex 61) where it means 'expert advice'.

[2] III.xxiv. Cf. above, p. 16.

[3] Fr. 632 (Kock) (Ex 34 and 57), cited above, p 25, n. 1.

[4] *Or.* 396 (Ex 17 and 56), cited below, p. 47, n. 5: cf. also p. 26, n. 3, above.

goes on to describe in detail the nature of this suffering.[1] When, however, Stobaeus[2] in his turn excerpts the Plutarchian passage, he deletes the Euripidean line, as he has already excerpted it together with the line preceding it, and replaces it with τὸ συνειδός as the unambiguous one-word equivalent of the whole. That the extreme lateness of Stobaeus' *floruit* does not invalidate this as bearing on the usage at the earlier period in which St. Paul wrote, is shown not only by the fact that Plutarch usually uses τὸ συνειδός, and only replaces it with the Euripidean line as a literary flourish, so that the passage as amended by his excerptor is entirely consistent with his other references to the subject[3]; but also by a comparison of Philo with Polybius. The latter speaks of σύνεσις[4] in terms all but identical with those of the former's description of τὸ συνειδός.[5] For both writers, what is plainly the same experience, by whatever name either calls it, *dwells in the soul of every man* as a *fearful witness* and a *terrible accuser*.

So far, then, we have, via σύνεσις, established the equation αὐτῷ συνειδέναι = τὸ συνειδός. But our enquiry began from the observation that the Pseudo-Epictetus passage,[6] for the sake of variety, uses both συνείδησις and τὸ συνειδός as interchangeable. We may therefore take our equation as sufficiently established to justify an attempt to verify it by the simple experiment of converting a συνείδησις into a αὐτῷ συνειδέναι example. If the sense remain quite unaltered no further proof will be needed, although all the examples subsequently to be adduced will provide incidental corroboration for our conclusion.

Coriolanus, Dionysius of Halicarnassus[7] tells us, was hesitant in his approach to the Volsci. The unwarlike character of the

---

[1] Plutarch: *De Tranq. Anim.* 476F–477A (Ex 49), cited below, p. 47 f and note. I have included it under τὸ συνειδός for reasons that will be clear from the text above.
[2] *Op. cit.*
[3] Cf. also: *Quomodo quis suos in virtute sentiat profectus* 84D (Ex 50), cited below, p. 127; *De sera numinis vindicta* 556A (Ex 51), cited below, p. 34; and *Publicola* iv.99B (Ex 52), cited below, p. 115, n. 4.
[4] Polyb: XVIII.xliii.13 (Ex 58), cited below, p. 41, n. 1.
[5] Philo: *QDPIS* 23 (Ex 48), cited below, p. 41, n. 1; with which cf. *QDSI* 128 (Ex 47) cited below, p. 49. The verbal similarity between the two authors is so striking that it is easier to believe in the dependence of Philo on Polybius than in such a coincidence. If this is so Philo's change to τὸ συνειδός is deliberate and argues therefore the more strongly for our equation.
[6] Epict: Fr. 97 (Schweighaüser) (Ex 54 and 84), cited below, p. 51; cf. pp. 13 and 15, above, and notes.
[7] Dion. Halic: *Ant.* viii.1.3 (Ex 76).

then consuls would afford an opportunity for a reversal of his exile by force of arms. The sole sufficient force available–granted able leadership–is that of the Volsci, whom he hopes to induce not only to receive him amicably, but also to entrust to him the command of their army. His hesitation is due to συνείδησις which disquieted him in that he had many times inflicted terrible things on them in battle. The operative words in this passage are: ἐτάραττε αὐτὸν ἡ συνείδησις ὅτι δεινὰ δεδρακὼς ἦν αὐτους. Had Xenophon been the historian he would have written . . . αὐτοὺς δεινὰ δεδρακότι αὐτῷ συνειδὼς ἐταράσσετο. The meaning is exactly the same, and the usage is straightforwardly MBNorm.

It is thus plain both that συνείδησις (and τὸ συνειδός) is the substantival equivalent of τὸ αὐτῷ συνειδέναι, and that its usages are patient of the same system of classification. The verbal phrase and its construction are complex, so that the need for a substantival equivalent was bound to be soon felt, as Demosthenes shows by using the articular infinitive.[1] σύνεσις appears to have been used tentatively to begin with, but it was not sufficiently unequivocal and was soon ousted by συνείδησις and τὸ συνειδός,[2] as being obviously suitable, the former as from the same root as, and the latter as the articular participle of the verb concerned.

When, as is now possible, the M categories discovered by analysis of the use of the verbal phrase are transferred to the substantives, understanding is greatly assisted if the constructions used to express the content of that phrase be borne in mind. There are two such constructions, which are used interchangeably, largely for reasons either of syntactical convenience, or even of personal taste. They can of course also be used in combination.

Thus the content can be expressed: (i) by a noun or its equivalent, in the accusative as the object of συνειδέναι; or (ii) by a participle either (*a*) in the nominative agreeing with the subject of συνειδέναι, or (*b*) in the dative agreeing with the reflexive pronoun. If (iii) the two are used in combination, then the noun, or its equivalent, in the accusative is, of course, the object of the participle.

---

[1] Dem: *de Fals. Leg.* 208 (Ex 28), referred to p. 48 below.
[2] Cf. p. 19 f, above, for a suggestion concerning the relation between these two substantives.

As, further, the constructions (i) and (ii) are interchangeable, it is safe to observe that where the accusative noun appears alone, the participle may, at the very least for purposes of exegesis, be understood. This is clearly indicated by the invariable use of μὴ as the negative,[1] even in construction (i) in classical Greek. The reverse is equally true—that an active verb implies an accusative—but is less significant. What is significant is the tense[2] of the participle whenever it is expressed, and therefore to be inferred when unexpressed. It is an additional and important datum for a conclusion as to the nature of αὐτῷ συνειδέναι, and, obviously therefore, of συνείδησις as well.

The category into which a use of one or other of these substantives must fall is to be determined, as in the case of the verbal phrase, largely by the relation of their consequences[3] with their reference.[4] As the verb could have an object, and as in the participial construction the participle agreed with the subject or his dependent reflexive pronoun, it was possible to speak of its 'content'. The usage of the nouns however compels us to the less precise nomenclature of 'reference'.[4] For this reference is expressed in one of three ways[5]: (a) the genitive of some noun or its equivalent describing an act (or acts) disposition or condition. This is by far the most common and represents the content of αὐτῷ συνειδέναι—i.e. the object of συνειδέναι or the activity, etc., of its subject; (b) a subordinate clause or a prepositional phrase: this is infrequent but when used, also represents the content of αὐτῷ συνειδέναι; (c) an epithet agreeing with συνείδησις or τὸ συνειδός: this is only less uncommon than (b). When there are sufficient data for reasonable certainty in exegesis it is quite clear that this does not represent the content of αὐτῷ συνειδέναι but at most the condition of συνείδησις or τὸ συνειδός in relation to that content.

Understanding of the connotation of the nouns is often helped further by the application to them of a metaphor or simile.[6]

With such equipment it is easy to recognise MBA and MBNorm.

---

[1] οὐ is only used to negative an adjective where litotes is intended cf. p. 26, n. 3 above citing Eur: *Med.* 495 (Ex 18).

[2] See below on Nature (Reference) pp. 42 ff.

[3] Column VII of the analytical index to the nouns.

[4] Column V of the analytical index to the nouns.

[5] These statements are verifiable in detail by reference to the analytical index.

[6] Column VI of the analytical index to the nouns.

Democritus[1] gives a good example of the latter when he writes that the generality of mankind, in their ignorance of the dissolution of mortal nature, suffer wretchedly throughout their lifetime from distress and fear because of their συνείδησις of the evil-doing in their lives. It is to the combination of their ignorance with συνείδησις that he attributes their groundless speculations about the period after death.

In MBA, while either the consequences, the descriptions or both, of συνείδησις show it to be MB, no reference is explicitly stated–it being held sufficiently implied by the noun itself. So Plutarch conceives of the expulsion of τὸ συνειδός,[2] used absolutely, from the soul, as parallel both to its becoming pure, and to its escape from the memory of its past wrong acts. 'The soul of every wicked person will probably meditate thus (upon the empty joylessness of vice) and take counsel with itself how it may escape the memory of its ill-deeds, cast out τὸ συνειδός and, having become pure, live another life over again from the beginning.'[3]

The three phrases are not a mere tautology: each adds something to the description of the burden that must be disposed of. They interlock, rather than overlap. The evil acts, however long past, are still remembered because of τὸ συνειδός: and the memory of them is as effective in *arousing* (or, in view of *casting out*, perhaps better, *introducing*) τὸ συνειδός as were the acts themselves when

---

[1] Democritus 297 (Diels) (Ex 72): ἔνιοι θνητῆς φύσιος διάλυσιν οὐκ εἰδότες ἄνθρωποι, συνειδήσει δὲ τῆς ἐν τῷ βίῳ κακοπραγμοσύνης, τὸν τῆς βιοτῆς χρόνον ἐν ταραχαῖς καὶ φόβοις ταλαιπωροῦσι, ψεύδεα περὶ τοῦ μετὰ τὴν τελευτὴν μυθοπλαστέοντες χρόνου. I have paraphrased ἔνιοι by *the generality of* because it is plainly shown by *in their ignorance* . . . to be the intellectual's litotes for 'all mankind–except me and those who have grasped my doctrine'. The usage is MBNorm in that, with the addition only of αὐτοῖς, were συνειδήσει replaced with συνειδότες and the genitive by an accusative the sense would be quite unaltered. Possibly the unhappy conjunction . . . εἰδότες, συνειδότες . . . influenced Democritus' preference for the noun. That this most distinguished of philosophers should use MBNorm rather than PTI is not surprising. The separation of these two uses is not clearly to be distinguished until Aristotle, even Plato using them indifferently side by side. In any case it is διάλυσις that is the philosophic concept here, as opposed to συνείδησις which Democritus scorns as popular. Cf. Norden's comment, p. 17, above. For ταραχή cf. Soc. ap Stobaeus, *loc. cit.* (Ex 9) cited below, p. 56. For the colouring of the whole of life by συνείδησις cf. Isoc: to Nicocles 59 (Ex 13). For the fear motif cf. refs. on p. 111 f and notes, below.

[2] The equivalence of the nouns is of course taken as proved in this chapter.

[3] Plutarch: *De sera numinis vindicta* 556A (Ex 51): ταῦθ' ἑκάστου τῶν πονηρῶν εἰκὸς τὴν ψυχὴν ἀναπολεῖν ἐν αὑτῇ καὶ διαλογίζεσθαι πῶς ἂν ἐκβᾶσα τῆς μνήμης τῶν ἀδικημάτων καὶ τὸ συνειδὸς ἐξ ἑαυτῆς ἐκβαλοῦσα καὶ καθαρὰ γενομένη βίον ἄλλον ἐξ ἀρχῆς βιώσειεν.

first committed. τὸ συνειδός works upon the soul in such a way as to make her express herself in the terms 'I am unclean'. The verbs used also can bear a little pressure. *Memory* is that in which the soul is confined (*escape from*)–her prison house. τὸ συνειδός is that which is in the soul–her feeling in reaction to imprisonment (*cast out*). *Unclean* is what she *is*–the cause of her imprisonment (*having become*).

When, however, due weight has been given to each portion of the clause, it is still a single event which will deliver the soul from its predicament: the three phrases if not exact equivalents are still three parallel aspects of the one event that is sought, and cannot be separated from it or from each other. The soul is only in one prison–her past life and her resultant character: and she desires release and takes counsel with herself how it may be achieved. For the present purpose it is sufficient to notice that τὸ συνειδός is the internal element of the soul's present distressful situation and that she desires to, rather *must*, cast this out, that she may start life anew. However much the context does in fact make its connotation clear as MB, the word itself is used absolutely.

While MBA is the most frequent M usage of τὸ συνειδός, MBNorm is of συνείδησις. MBNeg and MPG are uncommon of both words,[1] and are chronologically of doubtful significance for N.T. usage.[2] Although, further, they are readily distinguishable from either MBNorm or MBA, it is not always so easy to discern the one from the other.

When Heliodorus makes one of his characters say that if he can but deliver his charge safely into Theagenes' hands, he will have been manifestly a worthy guardian of that entrusted to him and can depart with good συνειδός[3] the usage is clearly MPG.

[1] The statistics are: (*a*) τὸ συνειδός; Total M examples: 19, of which 11 are MBA; 1 MBNorm; 2 (perhaps 4) MBNeg; 2 (possibly 4) MPG. The nineteenth is Stobaeus, a Chapter-heading only; cf. p. 16; (*b*) συνείδησις: Total M examples: 24, of which 11 are MBNorm; 7 MBA; 3 (probably 5) MBNeg; perhaps 2 MPG. The twenty-fourth is in itself unclassifiable.

[2] The earliest possible MPG use of τὸ συνειδός is later in date than the latest N.T. writing, and neither MBNeg use can be dated before the N.T., the earlier certainly being later than St. Paul's death. The possible MPG uses of συνείδησις while being ascribed to Bias and Periander do not appear in writing until *c.* A.D. 500. The MBNeg uses are all much later in origin than the N.T. Cf. Column III of the analytical index.

[3] Heliod: vi.7 (Ex 40): . . . μετὰ ἀγαθοῦ τοῦ συνειδότος χωριζοίμην. Cf. also Alciphron I.x.5 (Ex 38) wherein τὸ συνειδός of good deeds and good works is held to afford delight no less than a material reward.

Irrespective of the use of the epithet *good*,[1] the context shows that the content of τὸ συνειδός is a mission faithfully accomplished, and implies that with such a content it is itself sufficient reward for his trouble.

Should we be tempted by this to assume that the use of the epithet *good*[1] automatically indicates MPG, Herodian quickly disabuses us. For he uses the phrase in such a way as to leave no doubt whatever that he understood it as MBNeg, when he says that to shake one's self free of those who are troubling one while retaining a good συνείδησις affords one great confidence, and while one's self doing no wrong to defend (or, even, avenge) one's self is a source of cheerful hope.[2] The parallelism of this dictum is reminiscent of the Semitic literature,[3] and is of great relevance and interest to us now. *Cheerful hope* and *great confidence* are virtually synonyms: both stand for the notion expressed in English by such phrases as *good cheer* or *good heart*.[4] The difference between the two verbs is due entirely to a stylistic inversion of construction for the sake of variety: *great confidence* is the object of the first, and *cheerful hope* the subject of the second, of the two parallel clauses co-ordinated by *both . . . and*. Nor is there any real distinction of meaning between *to shake one's self free*, etc. and *to defend* (or *avenge*) *one's self*. From all this it must follow that here it is *one's self doing no wrong* that is the equivalent of *a good συνείδησις*. The problem envisaged is the perennial one. How is a man to worst his enemies without worsening himself, to defend himself against evil without recourse to the weapons of evil? In the solution of this problem, as Herodian rightly says, lies a good and cheerful outlook. He plainly thinks it can be done: Christianity, despite the countless attempts at evasion on the part of its adherents, holds plainly that it cannot, and should not be attempted. The wrongdoer can do one no essential harm unless

---

[1] ἀγαθός.

[2] Herodian: *Hist.* VI.iii.4 (Ex 69): . . . τὸ δὲ τοὺς ἐνοχλοῦντας ἀποσείεσθαι ἐκ τε τῆς ἀγαθῆς συνειδήσεως ἔχει τὸ θαρραλέον, καὶ ἐκ τοῦ μὴ ἀδικεῖν ἀλλ' ἀμύνεσθαι ὑπάρχει τὸ εὔελπι.

[3] This Semitic parallelism, together with the gnomic cast of the passage, may possibly lend support to the supposition of a Syriac origin for the author–a supposition which is not discredited by his name. Whether this be his own composition or a proverb appositely quoted–perhaps from youthful memory–is not here in point.

[4] θαρραλέος is used by Aeschylus (*Prom. V.*536) as an epithet of ἐλπίς and the two taken together are used as meaning (φανὴ) εὐφροσύνη and in opposition to the μυρίοι μόχθοι that Prometheus is suffering.

he can goad one into resistance, whereby one harms one's self. But this is not in point here. All that concerns us now is that the sentence is discussing not two problems, nor even two variations of the same problem, but one problem described twice with only slight variations of language. There is but one situation—a man is molested in some way by others—from which relief is sought. Such relief will only not turn to ashes in his mouth—will only provide the desired happiness—if it can be gained without his falling into wrongdoing and its consequent συνείδησις.

Thus it is plain that here by ἀγαθὴ συνείδησις Herodian means precisely τὸ αὐτῷ μηδὲν ἀδικῶν συνειδέναι. This is of course clearly MBNeg.

Of two examples both using the phrase ἀγαθὴ συνείδησις one is seen to be MPG because the author has definitely stated the content of συνείδησις; and this is true of the one other example which is undoubtedly MPG.[1] The other however, while no less decisively MBNeg, shows that its author used the phrase casually as self-explanatory—took MB, in fact, for granted as the norm and used *good* to supply the negative. The statement[2] that the epithet used of συνείδησις does not represent the content of αὐτῷ συνειδέναι is thus entirely justified. Where no content is expressed or even implied for συνείδησις[3] our sole internal guides for classification must be either its consequences or its description by simile or otherwise. But the consequences of both MBNeg and of MPG are virtually the same, and in none of the contentless examples[4] is any description given.

The category to which such examples belong must therefore, so far as we are dependent on internal guides, remain doubtful between MPG and MBNeg. I have included them all under

[1] Cf. p. 35, n. 3, above.   [2] Cf. p. 33, above.

[3] In the two very similar formulae, *Arch. Pap.* iii.418.13 (Ex 70) and *Pap. Par.* 21.15 (Ex 71) cited in parallel p. 126, n. 1, below, the context plainly implies that βεβαία (ἄδολος) συνείδησις represents αὐτοῖς μηδένα δόλον συνειδότες; cf. also *Orph. Hymn* lxiii.3 f (Ex 43) cited below p. 49, n. 14. In Jos: *Bell. Jud.* I.xxiii.3 (Ex 42): συνήργει δ' αὐτῷ μετὰ καθαροῦ τοῦ συνειδότος ἡ περὶ λόγους ἰσχύς–καθαρός is of course itself a negative word; cf. below, pp. 51 and 94.

[4] These are: of τὸ συνειδός: Paus. VII.x.10 (Ex 37): ὑπὸ συνειδότος ἐπαρρησιάζετο ἀγαθοῦ; and *Pap. Reinach*, lii.5 (Ex 39): ἠμελήσατε οὐ καλῷ συνειδότι χρώμενοι, and of συνείδησις; Periander ap Stobaeus, *loc. cit.* (Ex 67): ἀγαθὴ συνείδησις ... ἐστὶν ἐλευθερία, and Bias, *ibid*, (Ex 68): ὀρθὴ συνείδησις ... ἐστι τῶν κατὰ βίον ἄφοβον. The οὐ καλῷ in Ex 39 may indicate a litotes, in which case the use is MBNorm. If, however, οὐ negatives χρώμενοι, the whole clause being taken together, the passage is doubtful between MPG and MBNeg.

MPG both to avoid all suspicion of tendenciousness and more particularly to allow the fullest possible weight to MPG in arriving at the connotation of συνείδησις; but we are in point of fact very far from being dependent only on internal indications for our classifications. The available evidence taken as a whole must lead us to accept the *a priori* probability, in default of any clear indications to the contrary, of an MB interpretation of all these words. The statistics even alone are almost sufficient[1]: but they can do no more than corroborate a probability already overwhelming. For the existence of only one MBA[2] example, let alone a total of 24 out of 89 of which only 77 are M, would be sufficient indication that we must extend the conclusion already forced on us in the case of the verbal phrase[3] to the substantives also. They too 'expect the content *bad* unless, as is found very rarely, the opposite is explicitly stated'. The normal content of συνείδησις being thus *bad*, its condition will also normally be unhappy. Thus it is readily understandable that when συνείδησις is *empty*[4] it should be called *good*.[5] The MBA usage regards the content as necessarily *bad* if it arise to contain anything: so that it is at its best when containing nothing. To such general conclusions reached on the basis of examples in which συνείδησις is not used with an ambiguous epithet, Herodian[6] has enabled us to add the very strong corroboration of his passage in which it is so used.

It is not often that the pursuit of a Greek popular commonplace will be suddenly facilitated by the appearance of a Semitic parallelism that is above suspicion of distortion by Christian influence–a parallelism that permits a precise interpretation of a phrase in one part of the sentence by its parallel in the other half. It is therefore to be recorded, when such an opportunity has occurred, that it bears out fully these conclusions. It is perhaps far too strong to say that this one passage of Herodian proves conclusively that ἀγαθὴ συνείδησις and kindred phrases can only be interpreted in an MBNeg sense. On the other hand the least

---

[1] Cf. p. 22, n. 3, for the overall statistics of MB; p. 24, n. 5, for those of MBNorm of the verbal phrase; and p. 35, n. 1, for those of the substantives.

[2] Almost certainly the popular usage; cf. p. 27 f, above.   [3] Cf. p. 28, above.

[4] Cf. p. 26, above; the analogy of the empty bottle.

[5] Cf. p. 27 above, and n. 2 *i id*.

[6] *Hist.* VI.iii.4 (Ex 69) p. 36, above, cited n. 2.

that can possibly be inferred is that such phrases cannot be assumed to be necessarily MPG because of the epithet. When all the evidence there is points one way, but is slight in quantity and undistinguished in provenance, the fairest judgment that can be reached is a presumption, *ceteris paribus*, of the MBNeg interpretation. Unless the context in particular cases offers other evidence, ἀγαθὴ συνείδησις should usually be taken as the equivalent of τὸ αὐτῷ μηδὲν ⟨κακὸν⟩ συνειδέναι.[1]

[1] This conclusion will be found entirely supported by N.T. usage, cf. pp. 94 ff, below. In the verbal phrase MPG is an early stage of development; in the substantives it is very late. Cf. Column III of the analytical index: also p. 35, n. 2, and p. 45. It is probably logically as well as chronologically a development of the MBA usage. As in the case of the verbal phrase, that so obvious and legitimate a development should be so rare, and, of the nouns, so late, is of considerable significance to our present enquiry.

IV

THE MEANING OF συνείδησις

On the basis of the analysis in the last two chapters[1] it is now possible to set out as established a description of the idea connoted by συνείδησις in popular usage.[2] This is best done under three heads: its *nature*,[3] its reference and its function.

In nature, it can best be summed up, it is an element of human nature as such; but at the same time of human nature as integrally involved in an ordered universe. The three factors which go to make up this sum are: first, its connection with 'Ανάγκη–the fixed and determinate order of things-as-they-are. Socrates is content to let their own συνείδησις punish those who induced the witnesses at his trial to give perjured evidence against him, for he is satisfied that in the nature of things they will suffer greatly from such knowledge within themselves of sacrilege and injustice,[4] which will have followed automatically upon the act's commission.

But it is an element of 'Ανάγκη that resides in the nature of man as man–and this is the second factor: this is implicit in almost all examples and explicit in many. So Polybius asserts that there is

---

[1] Summarised in the analytical index at the end of this book.

[2] As opposed, of course, not to literary, but to philosophic and technical usage.

[3] Strictly, the 'nature' of συνείδησις is composed of these three heads together. By the first head is meant the place of συνείδησις in the created universe as a whole.

[4] Xen: *Apol.* 24 (Ex 23): 'Ανάγκη ἐστὶ πολλὴν ἑαυτοῖς ἀσέβειαν καὶ ἀδικίαν συνειδέναι. Cf. also Vett. Val. V.i. (Ex 85) cited below, p. 58, n. 6, in which, in connection with horoscopes, it is likened to the fixed geographical obstacles which to some extent dictate the course of the traveller. Stobaeus preserves (*loc. cit.*) in his catena a Sophoclean fragment which Dindorf wrongly, for they owe their survival solely to the excerptor, who separates them, includes as part of Fr. 669 in his *Poet. Scen. Graec.*, 2nd Edition:

κλέπτων δ' ὅταν τις ἐμφανῶς ἐφευρεθῇ
σιγᾶν ἀνάγκη, κἂν καλὸν φέρῃ στόμα.

This appearance of ἀνάγκη is the more significant as contained in a fragment which does not mention συνείδησις or any of its cognates and yet is included as illustrating τὸ συνειδός. For συνείδησις as enforcing silence cf. Dem: *de Fals. Leg.* 208 (Ex 28) referred to p. 48, below.

no witness so fearful, nor accuser so terrible as that σύνεσις which dwells in the soul of *every man*.[1]

From these two factors it is not difficult to foresee the emergence–in a suitable 'theological' climate–of the third–the tracing of συνείδησις to God [or the Gods] as the orderer of the universe. This is implicit in many writers, as needs no demonstration in the case of Philo,[2] who despite his veneer of Hellenistic philosophy, is a Jewish theologian through and through. It is more or less explicit when Xenophon brings it into relation with prayer and its response,[3] or supposes it so to intervene when sacred oaths are neglected as to make the forsworn accursed[4]: as well as when Democritus[5] asserts that in the popular mind it is connected with punishment after death. Two writers[6] in the interests of 'modernism' make it do duty for the Eumenides in their versions of popular legends.[7] It is fully explicit in Menander[8] who calls it, summarily, *divine*: the Pseudo-Epictetean fragment[9] goes into more detail, explicitly asserting (*a*) that God implants it in men; (*b*) that he hands them over to its guardianship; and, therefore, (*c*) that its enemies are at enmity with God also.[10]

[1] Polyb. XVIII.xliii.13 (Ex 58): οὐδεὶς οὕτως οὔτε μάρτυς ἐστὶ φοβερὸς οὔτε κατήγορος δεινός, ὡς ἡ σύνεσις ἡ κατοικοῦσα ἐν ταῖς ἑκάστων ψυχαῖς.
σύνεσις of course here=συνείδησις. Cf. p. 51, below: there we see also that Philo, allegorising the man who redirects the searching Joseph to Dothan (Gen. 37.15), refers to him as ἐν ἑκάστου ψυχῇ κατοικῶν and including in his functions those of τὸ συνειδός–'λαβὼν τάξιν μάρτυρος ἢ κατηγόρου ἔνδοθεν ἐλέγχει.' (*QDPIS* 23, Ex 48); cf. p. 58, n. 6. Cf. also Philo: *de Decalogo* 87, cited p. 47, below; Epict: Fr. 97 (Schweighaüser), Ex 54 and 84, cited p. 51, below; Menander: *Monost.* 654 (Ex 66), cited n. 8, below; Dem.: Fr. 297 (Diels) Ex 72, cited p. 34, above.
[2] Cf. Philo: *de Decalogo* 87, cited below, p. 47; *QDSI* 128 (Ex 47), cited below, p. 49; *QDPIS* 23 (Ex 48), cf. n. 1, above; Fr. (ed. Mang. II), p. 652 (Ex 46) and Fr. *ibid*, p. 659 (Ex 79), cited below, p. 49, n. 1, and p. 48, n. 7, respectively. Philo, whose floruit is *c*. A.D. 40, need not be supposed to have influenced directly any N.T. writer, but his works are admirable material for a picture of the field of ideas in which he and his contemporaries grazed, and of the sort of result to be expected from the impact of Hellenistic culture on the Hebrew tradition.
[3] Xen: *Cyr.* I.vi.4 (Ex 10), cited p. 25, above.
[4] Xen: *Anab.* II.v.7 (Ex 21), cited p. 24, above.
[5] Fr. 297 (Diels) (Ex 72), cited p. 34, above.
[6] Eur: *Or.* 395 f (Ex 17 and 56), cited below, p. 47, the *Oresteia* and Diod. Sic. iv.65 (Ex 78), cited below, p. 74, n. 3; the *Amphiaraos Legend*.
[7] Cf. also Vett. Val. V.i (Ex 85), cited below, p. 58, n. 6. Popular astrology then as now is a sort of debased surrogate theology.
[8] Men: *Monost.* 654 (Ex 66): βροτοῖς ἅπασιν ἡ συνείδησις θεός. It should be noticed that this monostich in isolation gives no clue whatever as to the reference or function of συνείδησις.
[9] Fr. 97 (Schweighaüser) (Ex 54 and 84), cited below, p. 51; cf. also p. 13, n. 10, above.
[10] Cf. also *Pap. Oxy.* II.218ᵃ.ii.19 (Ex 82) where the context is the selection of a

So much then for the nature of σuνείδησις. Going on to consider its M reference we find that it is always, first of all, to the quality of a man's own acts and, it follows, of his own character—that is, it is not concerned with the acts, attitudes or characters of others. This is certain, in that the reflexive pronoun is an integral and essential part of the verbal phrase represented—in its total connotation—by σuνείδησις. The σuν- of σύνοιδα governs the dative of the reflexive pronoun: the knowledge or awareness that a man has, the witness that he is in a position to bear—is internal. No external authority need be consulted: he knows, and is his own witness to himself; and this knowledge and witness are private to him alone. The constructions used in the verbal phrase are also relevant. We have seen[1] that even when its content is expressed by an accusative noun or its equivalent a participle may always be inferred. Whenever it occurs it is always in either the nominative or the dative. Of the two usages the former is the more common, but the choice between them never needs to be taken as more than a matter of style. Thus even were the use of the reflexive pronoun not in itself sufficient proof, the participle would still be complete demonstration that, whether nominative or dative be used, the subject of the act concerned is invariably the same as that of σuνειδέναι; for if the participle be in the dative it is so in agreement with the reflexive pronoun, itself of course referring to the subject of σuνειδέναι.[2]

Secondly its reference is to specific acts—and to character only in so far as that is both determined by and expressed in specific acts. This statement is perhaps less patient of exact demonstration than those above and below: but in support, it can be seen on the one hand that although frequently, particularly in the case of the substantives, there is no indication given, yet where there

---

priest of Ares in a trial by ordeal. Trials by ordeal, of course, presuppose a relationship between human morals and the behaviour of physical matter; this passage includes σuνείδησις within that relationship. In *Supp. Epigr.* IV.648.13 (Ex 81), cited below, p. 48, σuνείδησις is inflicted by the Gods as (inescapable) punishment; cf. also *Ath. Mitt.* xxiv.237 (Ex 89), cited below, p. 72.

[1] See p. 32 f, above, on construction. For tenses of the participle see pp. 43 ff, below.

[2] As σuνείδησις is in M uses the equivalent of τὸ αὐτῷ σuνειδέναι, the attempt to base on *etymological derivation* the interpretation of it as 'a knowing together with the will of God', as e.g. by Hallesby, *Conscience* (p. 10 of the English translation), must remain one of the curiosities of semasiological exegesis. For the theological truth underlying such an attempt cf. pp. 68 ff, below and *passim*.

are such indications they either–and this most often–bear the statement out, or, on occasion, are entirely neutral: while, on the other hand, the function of συνείδησις being as described below,[1] it is difficult to see what other reference it could have. In justification of the former claim the following rapid summary of the statistics may be advanced.

Of the M examples of αὐτῷ συνειδέναι those that employ the participial construction refer, naturally, to specific acts, while the MBNeg examples refer to the absence of such an act. Of the substantival construction only one example is indefinite[2]; the remainder refer to specific acts. The substantives frequently appear used absolutely,[3] or with an epithet. We have seen that in the latter use the epithet does *not* express the *content* of συνείδησις, so that neither of those two readily lend themselves to a specific reference. Despite this six MBA examples[4] do in fact refer to specific acts, or the condition which produces or results from them. All MBNorm examples of course have such a reference, and so in addition have three MPG examples.[5] The statistical case[6] is in fact overwhelming, and there is no need to point out in detail those 'indefinite' examples in which a specific reference is implied.

Thirdly, the reference is always to *past* acts. This we adumbrated above[7] in observing that, in the popular usage, αὐτῷ συνειδέναι was the result of a specific act as *antecedent* cause. There is no single case of the participial construction of αὐτῷ συνειδέναι that can bear any other interpretation. But it has already been observed[8] that the participial construction is always implied–the construction with the accusative being a mere alternative. There is, therefore, no evidence whatever to justify understanding the implied participle in any tense other than is actually found explicitly employed. And, as the equation τὸ αὐτῷ συνειδέναι = τὸ συνειδός = συνείδησις has been shown to be valid in every M

---

[1] Cf. pp. 51 ff.   [2] Soph: Fr. 669 (Dindorf), cited p. 23, above (Ex 7 and 35).
[3] I.e. MBA.
[4] Men: Fr. (Kock) 632 (Ex 34 and 57), cited above, p. 25; Plutarch: *Publicola* iv.99B (Ex 52), cited below, p. 115, n. 4; Herodian IV.vii.1 (Ex 59), cited below, p. 106, n. 5; *Pap. Ryl.* II.116.9 (Ex 86); *Pap. BGU*, IV.1024.iii.7 (Ex 88), cited below, p. 48, n. 9; *Ath. Mitt.* xxiv.237 (Ex 89), cited below, p. 72.
[5] Alciphron I.x.5 (Ex 38), cf. p. 35, n. 3, above. *Pap. Reinach* lii.5 (Ex 39), cf. p. 37, n. 4, above. Heliodorus vi.7 (Ex 40), cited above, p. 35
[6] The statistics are: of 77 M examples, 50 refer to specific acts: of the remaining 27, 8 are indefinite as being the epithetal use, and 19 the absolute use, including one chapter-heading.   [7] Cf. above, p. 28.   [8] Cf. above, pp. 32 f.

context,[1] this statement is as true of the substantives as of the verbal phrase. The statement, however, does require some further explanation.

In 'past acts' are included three alternatives, according to the tense of the participle. These are: (*a*) (aorist) an act or acts begun and completed in the past[2]; (*b*) (perfect) a present condition or character[3] resulting from an act completed in the past[4]; or (*c*) (present) a course of action continuing in the present and liable to continue into the future, but decisively begun in the past. In relation to any act the present tense cannot but imply the aorist of *begin*.[5] The difference between (*b*) and (*c*) is that it is possible to stop the course of action in (*c*) in which case the action will take on the character of (*a*); unless by so stopping the act is left unfinished, when all that will remain is the *having begun*. The man who is choking another to death is certainly guilty of the act of having begun to murder. If he relent in time for his victim to recover, that remains the whole of his guilt in this particular. He is not a murderer. The act in (*b*) on the other hand is irrevocably complete. The difference between (*a*) and (*b*) is perhaps not of great importance: every past act issues in a moral condition or character, so long as there is choice, whether it continues in a present course of action or not. If any significance is to be attributed to the choice of tense, it is perhaps that the perfect is preferred for the more heinous crimes, from the guilt of which the passage of time affords little relief. The criminal is, as a result of such a crime, more obsessed with its after-effects upon himself than with the act. This distinction cannot, of course, be pressed. Nevertheless it is plain that whereas a man might say 'I have stolen' or 'I once stole something', rather than 'I am a thief', he is more likely to say 'I am a murderer [or perjurer]' than 'I killed a man [or broke an oath] once', in answer to the question 'Why art thou so heavy O my soul, and why art thou so disquieted within me?'[6]

All the evidence in fact shows that συνείδησις must always be,

---

[1] Cf. above, pp. 29-32.   [2] E.g. Xen: *Cyr.* I.vi.4 (Ex 10), cited p. 25, above.
[3] Cf. observations on the relation of character to acts on pp. 42 f, above and just below.
[4] E.g. Xen: *Anab.* II.v.7 (Ex 21), cited p. 24, above. So Orestes, in Eur: *Or.* 395 f (Ex 17 and 56), cited below, p. 47, *having* killed Clytaemnestra, *is* a matricide.
[5] Cf. Xen: *Cyr.* I.v.11 (Ex 8), cited above, p. 23; N.B. particularly ἀρξάμενοι . . . ὄντες.   [6] Ps. 43.5.

by however little, subsequent to the act to which it refers—
whether that act be merely the embarkation on a long process
or instantly complete in itself.

The reference of συνείδησις, then, is to the specific *past* act or
acts, in the senses defined, committed by the *subject himself*. There
is also however one other element of its reference which is vitally
significant: normally the act, acts, condition or character are *bad*.
Neither the data in the analytical index, nor the demonstration
above[1] that the MB interpretation was all but certainly correct of
every use of a word in the συνείδησις family, need much ampli-
fication at this stage. MB is the norm: MBA could not exist
were this not so,[2] and in MBNeg it is always the σύνοιδα embedded
in συνείδησις that is negatived. It is not a case of litotes: to
trespass prematurely on 'function', συνείδησις comes into operation, it may be so expressed, on commission of a bad act. When
no such act has been committed, it remains dormant.

No example of συνείδησις could be certainly classified as MPG,
nor could any at all of σύνεσις. The rare MPG examples of the
verbal phrase are all at least 350 years earlier than the N.T.: of
those of τὸ συνειδός none is earlier than 100 years after it.[3] For
the N.T. period, therefore, it is safe to say that in popular usage—
in default of unequivocal indication to the contrary—συνείδησις is
concerned only with bad acts, conditions, or character.

The function of συνείδησις in its normal use can be expressed
in three slightly different ways, but the notion fundamental to
them all is that of pain. This is plain from the result[4] for its sub-

[1] Pp. 37-39.
[2] Cf. Ar: *Eq.* 184 (Ex 33). Demosthenes exhorts the sausage-seller to seek public
office, for which he is 'admirably qualified'–a loud-mouthed rogue, a 'spiv' and a
'wide boy'. He however doubts his capacity for such distinction. 'Oh dear', replies
Demosthenes, 'why do you say that? ξυνειδέναι τί μοι δοκεῖς σαυτῷ καλόν.' The
bitter irony of this comment on the corruption of contemporary Athenian politics
depends on the audience knowing that the 'proper content' of αὑτῷ συνειδέναι is
κακόν, and so understanding the reference to the gross reversal of values. Aristophanes probably has the same intention in *Vesp.* 999 (Ex 19) where criticism of
the juror system is conveyed by making acquittal of a prisoner, regardless of the
case for or against him, the content of αὑτῷ συνειδέναι, i.e. a crime in itself–but it is
less definite and I have retained it under MBNorm. MB has to be the Norm for
popular speech for such extreme uses of MBA to make their point. Cf. also above
p. 25, n. 1.
[3] For the detailed statistics see p. 35, nn. 1 and 2, above and references *ibid.* n. 3.
[4] Column VIII of the analytical index on the verbal phrase; Column VII in the
case of the nouns. The result of MBNeg of course has to be reversed, cf. p. 26 ff,
particularly p. 27, n. 2; p. 37 f, and p. 47.

ject attributed to συνείδησις by Greek authors. Wherever such a result is stated,[1] or may be inferred from the description of συνείδησις by simile or some other means, it is always a greater or less pain, defined often in the strongest terms–a crippling or disabling thing.

> . . . It is born with every soul and makes its abode with it, nor is it wont to admit therein anything that offends. Its property is ever to hate the evil and love the good. This same thing is at once both accuser and judge. When once stirred up, as accuser it lays charge, it makes accusation, it puts to shame: then again as judge it teaches, warns, counsels the soul to repent. If its suasions but prevail, joyfully it is reconciled. But if it cannot prevail, it gives not peace, but makes war. Never does it depart by day nor by night, but it stabs as with a goad, and inflicts wounds that know no healing, until it snap the thread of that soul's pitiful and accursed life.

In this moving description Philo[2] expresses himself in terms of the second of the three different ways in which the function of συνείδησις is described. For it can be said: (*a*) to be a pain; (*b*) to inflict pain, as here, and (*c*) to feel pain. (*b*) and (*c*) are derived from (*a*); for just as (*b*) arises from the expression of (*a*) in terms of the metaphor of person, so (*c*) is its expression in quasi-scientific categories as a faculty or organ of the individual.

---

[1] Only in five MB cases is no 'result' stated or implied. One of these is Stobaeus' (*loc. cit.* Ex 41) chapter-heading. Men: *Monost.* 654 (Ex 66), cited p. 41, above, has no room for its statement. In Ar: *Thesm.* 477 (Ex 20) the speaker's claim ἐμαυτῇ σύνοιδα is fraudulent: but he is none the less trying to awake συνείδησις in his hearers to paralyse their action against his master. Eur: *Or.* 395 f (Ex 17 and 56) cited below, p. 47, speaks so strongly of it as a pain that we may safely infer this in his *Med.* 495 (Ex 18) cited above, p. 26, n. 3. In the remaining case, *Pap. Oxy.* vi.898[20] (Ex 32), we would not perhaps, then, overstrain probability in suggesting that it is not stated because it could be taken for granted as painful.

[2] *de Decalogo* 87. This telling description is of ὁ ἔλεγχος. Comparison of it however with his descriptions of τὸ συνειδός (see references, p. 41, n. 2, above) show conclusively that they were for the author one and the same thing. Cf. particularly *QDSI* 128 (Ex 47 cited below, p. 49), where τὰ ὑπαίτια–the word I have rendered above by *anything that offends*–is defined as meaning τὰ τὸ συνειδός βαρὺν κατήγορον ἔχοντα. *Accuser* in the passage above is of course κατήγορος. *QDSI* goes on to describe τὸ συνειδός further as τὸν κατὰ ψυχὴν δικαστήν (the *judge* in the Decalogo passage is δικαστής); with κατὰ ψυχήν cf. de Decalogo's ἑκάστῃ ψυχῇ συμπεφυκώς καὶ συνοικῶν. The obvious conclusion here that, for Philo, ὁ ἔλεγχος = τὸ συνειδός is borne out by his use of ἐλεγχόμενα (as synonym for ὑπαίτια) in the same passage, and by equally striking similarities of language in the other passages referred to, p. 41, above, particularly *QDPIS* 23 (Ex 48), cited above, p. 41, n. 1.

That it is a pain is still the basic experience of the three: it is also the basis on which the dependent experiences are built. Thus while MBNorm and MBA are pain, MBNeg is the absence of such pain. But absence of pain is itself a pleasure, albeit a negative one. It is a short step from–to advance a parallel experience in illustration–the negative 'I do not feel ill–how pleasant!' to the positive 'I am in good health.' It is surprising therefore that, in the case of the συνείδησις group, this step was so seldom taken by Greek writers.[1] The glowing accounts[2] given of the pleasure resulting from the absence of συνείδησις are readily explicable by the contrast with the results of its normal operation.

As the function of συνείδησις can be described in these three ways, Plutarch's description of it by the metaphor of an ulcer[3] is admirable, for an ulcer can also be spoken of in such terms. Primarily it is a disease,[4] itself a painful thing; but it also torments him on whom it has developed: and it is further an extremely sensitive area that will recognise and react against injurious matter immediately. Euripides[5] describes συνείδησις as a disease from which Orestes suffers as a result of his terrible crime, and which is destroying him. Plutarch[6] takes the second line of this distich to replace his usual τὸ συνειδός and goes on to depict it as:

> like an ulcer in the flesh. It implants in the soul a remorse which never ceases to wound and goad it. Any other pain can be reasoned away, but this remorse is inflicted by reason, on the soul which is so racked with shame, and self-chastised. For just as those overcome by shivering-fits, or burning with fever, suffer worse and are in greater distress than those who suffer the equivalent, but external, heat or cold, so the pains which

[1] For the rarity of MPG, particularly in N.T. times, cf. p. 23, p. 39 and p. 45 above, particularly the statistical and chronological summaries on p. 35, nn. 1 and 2.
[2] I.e. MBNeg; cf. refs. on p. 27, n. 2, above. Intermediate between such glowing accounts and the painful results of MBNorm/MBA are Socrates ap Stobaeus (*loc. cit.* Ex 9) cited below, p. 56, n. 1; Isoc: *to Philip* 79 (Ex 12): *Syll* 567.7 (Ex 16) and *Pap. Reinach* lii.5 (Ex 39), cited above, p. 37, n. 4 (if this be MBNeg) in which the result stated or inferrable is no more than the absence of pain.
[3] ἕλκος: for ref. see n. 6, below.
[4] as in Eur: *Or.* 395 f (Ex 17 and 56), cited immediately below.
[5] Eur: *Or.* 395 f (Ex 17 and 56).
    Menelaus: τί χρῆμα πάσχεις; τίς σ᾽ ἀπόλλυσιν νόσος;
    Orestes: ἡ σύνεσις, ὅτι σύνοιδα δείν᾽ εἰργασμένος.
[6] *de Tranq. Animi* 476F–477A (Ex 49). The passage is too long to cite in full, but N.B.: ὁ λόγος ἀναιρεῖ ἄλλας λύπας. Cf. p. 31, above, for reasons for including this under τὸ συνειδός in the analytical index.

come as it were from without and by chance are more easy to bear. But the cry

'None other is to blame for this but I myself'

coming from within upon the wicked man's own sins, makes his sufferings yet harder to bear.

What is stated here by Plutarch so explicitly as to be somewhat laboured is no more than the idea that underlies every use of the συνείδησις group of words. Of no MB example whatever can it be said that such an idea was not in its author's mind, and in the majority there are at least echoes of Plutarch's language.

Xenophon says that the sufferer from it can never again be counted happy, and makes Socrates declare that its pains are in themselves sufficient punishment for whatever crime it may refer to.[1] Isocrates says that it is as much to be feared as the results of the discovery of one's crime by others.[2] Demosthenes describes it as paralysing in its effects, and as full of fear and trembling as the expectation of blows.[3] The boldest, says Menander, is reduced to the extremes of terror by it.[4] Stobaeus, rightly or wrongly, supposes Sophocles to call it *a terrible thing*[5]; there is no hope of a new start in life, nor can the soul become stainless, until it be cast out.[6] It is sufficient vengeance on the wicked says Philo[7] for it is a chastisement from which there is no escape,[8] and the leader must walk in dread of it[9]: but such illustrations could be multiplied almost indefinitely.[10]

So much for descriptions of it as a pain. But many writers, often the same as those quoted above, also refer to it as the 'agent' by whom chastisement, forcible restraint, or both,[11] is inflicted. The metaphors both of *judge* and of *prosecutor* are fre-

---

[1] Xen: *Anab.* II.v.7 (Ex 21), cited above p. 24; and *Apol.* 24 (Ex 23), cited above, p. 40. [2] Isoc: *to Demonicus* 16 (Ex 27), cited below, p. 74, n. 1.

[3] Dem: *de Fals. Leg.* 208 (Ex 28): ... ἀποστρέφει τὴν γλῶτταν, ἐμφράττει τὸ στόμα. ἄγχει, σιωπᾶν ποιεῖ; and *de Corona* 263 (Ex 30).

[4] Men: Fr. 632 (Kock) (Ex 34 and 56), cited above, p. 25.

[5] *Loc. cit*: Soph: Fr. 669 (Dindorf) (Ex 35), cited above, p. 23, n. 6ᵃ.

[6] Plutarch: *de sera numinis vindicta* 556A (Ex 51), cited above, p. 34.

[7] Fr. *ed.* Mang. II, p. 659 (Ex 79): ἱκανὸς πρὸς τιμωρίαν ἡ τοῦ φαύλου συνείδησις, δειλίαν προτείνουσα τῇ ψυχῇ.

[8] *Supp. Epig.* IV.648.13 (Ex 81): ... ἐν συνειδήσι ... οἱ θεοὶ αὐτὴν ἐποίησαν ἐν κολάσει ἣν οὐ διέφυγεν.

[9] *Pap. BGU* IV.1024.iii.7 (Ex 88): ὁ ἡγεμὼν αἰδέσθητι ... τὴν συνείδησιν.

[10] see Column VIII on αὐτῷ συνειδέναι, and Columns VI and VII on the substantives in the analytical index.

[11] I.e. κόλασις which bears both senses.

quent. Philo refers to the sufferer as *self-condemned*[1]; the cause within him of his suffering is συνείδησις, the *stern accuser*, as well as the *judge*, and even the *witness* by whom his acts as well as himself are *censured* and he himself held in check as by bit and bridle.[2] It *chastises* from within, and *gnaws*, according to Plutarch[3]; and thus drives to such action as may appease it.[4] It forces bluntness on the speaker, as a judge demands truthfulness in the lawcourts.[5] It protects from harm like, and by sanctions similar to those of, the nursery-slave.[6] Fear of it deters from perjury.[7] Democritus sneers that the mass of men are compelled by it to pass wretched lives beset by tormenting fear.[8] According to Vettius Valens it constrains or restrains[9]: it disquiets according to Dionysius of Halicarnassus.[10] Diodorus Siculus substitutes it for the Eumenides in the *Amphiaraos* legend, as does Euripides in the *Oresteia*–for it too can drive the guilty man mad,[11] just as Philo thinks of it as injecting fear into the soul.[12] It can also persecute and by its goading incite to violence.[13]

If the distinction between συνείδησις as a pain, and as the 'agent' of its infliction is very fine, there is little more difference between them and its third conception–as the 'organ' or 'faculty' in which pain is felt. The Orphic hymn[14] speaks of it as that

---

[1] Philo: Fr. *ed.* Mang. II, p. 652 (Ex 46): μήποτε αὐτοκατάκριτος ἐν τῷ συνειδότι εὑρεθῇς. This is plainly the meaning of Marc. Aurel. 30 cited above, p. 146.

[2] Philo *QDSI.* 128 (Ex 47): τὰ ἀκούσια ἀνυπαίτια, τὸ συνειδὸς βάρυν κατήγορον οὐκ ἔχοντα, κτλ; cf. p. 46, n. 2, above. Also *QDPIS* 23 (Ex 48) cited p. 58, n. 6.

[3] κολάζειν and δάκνειν both appear in *de Tranq. Anim.* 476F-477A (Ex 49), cited above p. 47 f; and δάκνειν in *Quomodo quis suos in virtute sentiat profectus* 84D (Ex 50) cited below, p. 127. Cf. also Vett. Val. V.i (Ex 85), cited below, p. 58, for κολάζειν.

[4] Plutarch: *Publicola* iv.99B (Ex 52); cf. also Herodian IV.vii.1 (Ex. 59), both cited below, p. 115 and 106 respectively.

[5] Dio Chrysostom: *Corinthiaca* 35 (Ex 53).

[6] Epict.: Fr. 97 (Schweighaüser) (Ex 54 and 84), cited below p. 51.

[7] *OGIS* 484.37 (Ex 55), cited below, p. 50.

[8] Fr. 297 Diels (Ex 72), cited above, p. 34.

[9] V.i (Ex 85), cited below, p. 58: συνέχει or κατέχει. Cf. also *Test XII Patr: Reub.* iv.3 (Ex 73).

[10] ἐτάραττε: Dion. Halicarn: *Ant.* viii.1.3 (Ex 76), cited above, p. 31 f.

[11] Diod. Sicul: iv.65 (Ex 78), cited below, p. 74; Eur: *Or.* 395 f (Ex 17 and 56), cited above, p. 47.

[12] Fr. ed. Mang. II, p. 659 (Ex 79), cited above, p. 48.

[13] *Pap. Ryl.* II.116.9 (Ex 86).

[14] *Orph. Hymn* LXIII 3 f (Ex 43):
> . . . Δικαιοσύνη μεγαλαυχής
> ἣ καθαραῖς γνώμαις ἀεὶ τὰ δέοντα βραβεύεις
> ἄθραυστος τὸ συνειδός· ἀεὶ θραύεις γὰρ ἅπαντας
> ὅσσοι μὴ τὸ σὸν ἦλθον ὑπὸ ζυγόν.

The respect in which Justice is *unbroken* being τὸ συνειδός obviously the respect

aspect of personality in which it is possible to be *broken*–the accusative of respect being used of it, and Justice being personified. Those examples that use the phrase κατὰ συνείδησιν[1] and perhaps that which uses διὰ συνείδησιν[2] are at least patient of such interpretation. Certainly the assertion that deliberate falsehood defiles the συνείδησις of the historian,[3] can only be so understood.

What arises from this description of συνείδησις as, basically, a pain has already been briefly anticipated.[4] Until bad action has been committed, or at least initiated, there is no συνείδησις. If the secondary metaphors of internal agent or capacity be employed, the absence of the pain will have to be expressed in some such way as: 'συνείδησις is quiet', 'not aroused', or 'off duty'; but such phrases are doubly metaphorical, in that they themselves depend on metaphors.

The fundamental connotation of the συνείδησις group of words is that man is by nature so constituted that, if he overstep the moral limits of his nature he will normally feel pain–the pain called συνείδησις. Locomotion in any direction always involves the risk of at some time dashing the foot against a stone: normal experience will include many such foot-dashings, so that it is an adult as well as an instinctive piety to give thanks, to whatever power is conceived of as having the oversight of travelling, whenever a journey is accomplished without mishap: just as to wish an intending traveller 'a good journey' is a standard courtesy in every age. Even so, to action of any sort attaches a similar risk–for human action can never be entirely without moral significance. The wise and experienced will therefore rejoice when-

---

in which she *breaks* is the same. Those so *broken* are those who have not yet taken her yoke upon them, are not yet δίκαιοι, i.e. the ἄδικοι. The implicit τὸ συνειδός in the relative clause is thus equivalent to αὐτοῖς ἀδικίαν συνειδέναι, and so MBNorm; cf. Xen: *Apol.* 24 (Ex 23) cited above, p. 40; and Dem: *de Corona* 263 (Ex 30), etc., for details of the mode of this *breaking*. ἀθραυστος τὸ συνειδός thus means αὐτῇ μηδὲν ἄδικον συνειδυῖα and is MBNeg; cf. Plato: *Rep.* 331ᵃ (Ex 11) and *Syll* 567.7 (Ex 16). Justice is definitely personified here, and is the agent of βραβένεις and of θραύεις: τὸ συνειδός is specifically neither her internal counterpart, nor her assistant in these two functions, but solely the seat of θραῦσις. Her βραβεία is exercised by means of καθαραῖς γνώμαις.

[1] Hero: *Vet. Mech. Op.* (Paris 1693), p. 122.2 (Ex 83); Vett. Val. V.i (Ex 85) cited below, p. 58.
[2] *OGIS* 484.37 (Ex 55): διὰ τοῦ συνειδότος ὀμνύναι μὴ δυναμένους.
[3] Dion. Halicarn: *de Thuc. jud.* viii.3 (Ex 75): . . . ἑκουσίως ψεύδεσθαι . . . μιαίνειν τὴν αὐτοῦ συνείδησιν. [4] P. 45 above.

ever an action is accomplished, or initiated, without the ensuing onset of the moral foot-dashing, which is συνείδησις. If the 'goodness' of a journey lies in the absence of mishap, or even discomfort, the absence of συνείδησις is taken as a great joy.[1] This absence is classically expressed by μηδὲν αὑτῷ συνειδέναι— and it is a good and desirable thing. When the substantives replace the verbal phrase, it requires but the introduction of one or other of the two secondary metaphors for this 'good and desirable thing' to be expressed in, apparently, positive terms. In order that the reference to the absence of συνείδησις, rather than of any other sort of pain, may be made clear, συνείδησις has, paradoxically, to be included. Thus μηδὲν αὑτῷ συνειδέναι is represented in substantival form by such phrases as καθαρὰ συνείδησις (this is simple enough: the 'organ' metaphor, but the organ is empty, as the alimentary canal by fasting or purging), ἀγαθή or ὀρθὴ συνείδησις.

We have seen[2] that, particularly in the N.T. period, such phrases are, unless the opposite be explicitly stated, always MBNeg: that is, that συνείδησις, being, basically, a pain, ἡ ἀγαθὴ συνείδησις is, basically, the absent συνείδησις, and that it must be so understood, wherever the details of the particular context do not explicitly demand an MPG interpretation.

Our study of the Pagan-Greek background of the N.T.'s συνείδησις cannot do better than end where it began—with the fragment wrongly attributed to Epictetus by Meibomius.

'When we were children our parents handed us over to a nursery-slave who should watch over us everywhere lest harm befall us. But when we are grown up, God hands us over to the συνείδησις implanted in us, to protect us. Let us not in any way despise its protection, for should we do so we shall be both ill-pleasing to God and have our own συνειδός as an enemy.[3]

---

[1] Cf. Antiphanes ap Stobaeus, *loc. cit.* (Ex 14). ἡδονὴν πολλήν.

[2] Pp. 37-39, 45, above.

[3] Fr. 97 (Schweighaüser) (Ex 54 and 84): παῖδας μὲν ὄντας ἡμᾶς οἱ γονεῖς παιδαγωγῷ παρέδοσαν, ἐπιβλέποντι πανταχοῦ πρὸς τὸ μὴ βλάπτεσθαι· ἄνδρας δὲ γενομένους ὁ Θεὸς παραδίδωσι τῇ ἐμφύτῳ συνειδήσει φυλάττειν. ταύτης οὖν τῆς φυλακῆς μηδαμῶς καταφρονητέον, ἐπεὶ καὶ τῷ Θεῷ ἀπάρεστοι, καὶ τῷ ἰδίῳ συνειδότι ἐχθροὶ ἐσόμεθα.

With ἐμφύτῳ may be compared Philo's συμπεφυκὼς καὶ συνοικῶν as epithets of ὁ ἔλεγχος, as also his κατοίκουν of τὸ συνειδός, the thing governed by the συν- in the first case being ἑκάστῃ ψυχῇ; in the second case the κατοίκουν is explained by ἐν ἑκάστου τῇ ψυχῇ. Philo: cf. *de Decalogo* 87 with *QDPIS* 23 (Ex 48), see p. 41, n. 1,

The author of this fragment—much as Philo—regards συνείδησις as natural to man as man: but he has to make explicit what Philo can take for granted—that this means that it is implanted by God. Although it is perhaps elliptically stated, this is undoubtedly the sense—God having implanted συνείδησις hands us over to it. His conception of the purpose for which God implanted συνείδησις, and makes men its 'wards' also differs in no wise, either from Philo's or from that of any MB or even M example. Its function is to be likened to that of the nursery-slave, whose 'duty was rather to guard [his charges] from evil both physical and moral, than to communicate instruction, to cultivate their mind or to impart accomplishments. . . . The formation of their morals by direct superintendence belonged to the παιδονόμοι as public officers, and their instruction in the various branches of learning to the διδάσκαλοι'.[1]

We need have no hesitation in pressing the exact nature of this office for the elucidation of the present example, as the author quite deliberately does so himself, as *lest harm befall us . . . to protect . . .* and *its protection* plainly show. The proper office of the συνείδησις for which God implants it in man, is to protect him from harm, physical and moral, and not to teach, either morals or anything else. Of course much is in fact learnt about morals by simple experience of the things from which, by his intervention, the παιδαγωγός protects his charges. But such a process, as every wise nursemaid knows, exceeds its terms of reference and is in great danger of doing harm, when it forgets its negative character. The nursery-slave will leave his charges alone, merely maintaining a watchful eye, so long as their behaviour is physically safe and morally good: he will only step in when they have at least embarked on a course of action which leads into one or other sort of danger. He may thus on occasion be too late—the course of action between embarkation and accomplishment being short—to do anything but inflict penalties and point the moral: but to attempt to do more is to forget his place. The best he can

above. It is not only the happy variation of his παιδαγωγός theme (Gal. 3.24) which makes this fragment reminiscent of St. Paul, but also the final warning's close affinity with Rom. 13.5 (cf. below, pp. 71 f).

[1] Yates, citing Plato: *Rep.* i, p. 87; *de Leg.* vii, pp. 41, 42; *Lysis*, p. 118 all in ed. Bekker; Xen: *de Lac Rep.* ii.1, iii.12; Plutarch: *de Lib. Ed.* 7 and Quintilian: *Inst. Or.* i.1.8, 9; all as expressly distinguishing these three offices; in *Dictionary of Greek and Roman Antiquities*, ed. W. Smith, *ad loc.*

hope for is that his charges may have so learnt by previous and possibly painful experience the sort of acts that will rouse him to intervene, and may be so convinced of his ineluctable vigilance, as by their very fear of this intervention to be persuaded to maintain good and safe behaviour.

Such according to this fragment is the nature and function of συνείδησις: we have already seen that such a conception is in full accord with the general tenor of this word–together with those others of the same family examined–as it is found in the usage of the Greek-speaking man-in-the-street, constantly and without significant variation, throughout the history of the Greek language, to a point at least long after the period during which the N.T. was being written.

V

συνείδησις IN THE OLD TESTAMENT AND APOCRYPHA

THE stage is now reached, Greek popular usage having been analysed and conclusions drawn, for an enquiry into the usage of συνείδησις in the Bible. Following the English versions we may henceforward render it *conscience*, so long as we remember that it comes into Christianity directly and entirely from the everyday speech of the ordinary Greek. But it comes complete with its own connotation, as, basically, the pain suffered by man, as man, and therefore as a creature involved in the order of things, when, by his acts completed or initiated, he transgresses the moral limits of his nature.[1] Our enquiry so far has shown to be fully justified the standard conclusion of scholars as to the Greek understanding of conscience; that it is always or almost always a *guilty* conscience, and that all the Greek words for it look with scarcely an exception to 'conscience–the judge' and are primarily connected with shame. More than this, not only are we in a position to amplify and more closely to define this judgment in some significant particulars, but we also have evolved a system of analysis[2] which may illuminate the N.T. usage when applied to it.

We said at the outset that συνείδησις makes virtually its first Biblical appearance in the N.T. The qualification implied in *virtually* must now be somewhat expanded.

It was found that on occasion–although but rarely–σύνεσις could be used as a synonym for συνείδησις. This is a word that is very frequent in the Septuagint–as well as in the N.T.–but it appears always to be used in its ordinary sense. Its use to mean *conscience* is very far from being its primary sense in any case[3]:

---

[1] For an attempt to analyse the nature of this pain see pp. 111 ff, below.
[2] Cf. the analytical index of Greek sources at the end of this book.
[3] Cf. above, pp. 19 and 32.

its Biblical usage is, throughout, to mean simply *understanding*.[1]

The other–and very common synonym· for συνείδησις–τὸ συνειδός–does not appear at all in Bible or Apocrypha.

This study is not materially concerned with the simple σύνοιδα as it is only when this verb is used in construction with the dative of the reflexive pronoun that it is the verbal equivalent of *conscience*. In any case this verb is sufficiently rare in the Bible. N.T. examples have already been enumerated[2] with such little comment as is required. In the O.T. it occurs once[3] where it appears to connote such direct personal knowledge as would constitute the knower a witness–but obtained in some other way than by seeing. It also occurs twice perhaps in the Apocrypha–both times in the Maccabean saga.[4] A third appearance is also made in III Maccabees.[5] In none of the three cases does it mean much, if anything, more than συνιδόντες.[6]

The construction of σύνοιδα that is germane to our enquiry, that with the dative of the reflexive pronoun, occurs twice in the Greek Bible: once in the LXX and once in the N.T.[7] This latter will be examined later. The LXX passage is of great significance in that its rendering–'I do not know with myself that I have done anything amiss'[8]–is nothing that can be called a translation of the Hebrew. This is of course only to be expected in this book: for 'the character of the [LXX] translation is too free and loose to be of much service in the detailed criticism of the text'.[9] Criticism of the text is not our present purpose, so that we can feel unmixed gratitude to the translator for his freedom and looseness. His clause 'paraphrases' the second half of the verse which in the R.V. reads 'My heart shall not reproach me so long as I live.' 'Paraphrase' hardly does the translator justice: what he has done is completely to interpret the underlying notion of the Hebrew into a Greek commonplace. For this sentence as it stands is a flawless example of the MBNeg usage with which we are

---

[1] Cf. above, p. 19, n. 1.　　　[2] Cf. above, p. 18.　　　[3] Lev. 5.1.

[4] I Mac. 4.21; II Mac. 4.41.　　　[5] III Mac. 2.8.

[6] Indeed some MSS. prefer to read it so in each case. Thus in I Mac. 4.21 while συνειδότες is read by Alexandrinus alone; Sinaiticus and the Sixtine edition prefer συνιδόντες. In II Mac. 4.41 Alexandrinus is quite alone in its preference for συνειδότες, and in III Mac. 2.8 the Sixtine. In general in the Maccabean books συνιδόντες is the undisputed reading.

[7] I Cor. 4.4. See below, pp. 65 and 88 ff.

[8] Job 27.6: οὐ γὰρ σύνοιδα ἐμαυτῷ ἄτοπα πράξας.

[9] Davison: art. 'Job' in *Hastings Dictionary of the Bible*.

already perfectly familiar.[1] Two points of particular interest are: firstly, that, here the negative is unequivocally attached to σύνοιδα; that in MBNeg this was its idiomatic application was the conclusion demanded by the analysis of the evidence.[2] The Greeks however in general preferred to express this by the neater turn of phrase putting μή or one of its compounds with the participle implied or expressed rather than οὐ with the main verb: but the translator here with his clumsier expression has extracted the essence of what the usage implies: and secondly, in that the idea he expresses is one of internal reproach, the translator in his choice of phrase makes it clear that what this study has called MBNorm, is in fact the norm for him.

English idiom is not so different from the Greek that it is impossible to find at this stage an English equivalent for such verbal usage. Conscience being normally a pain, and its negative being, obviously, the absence of such pain, when nothing wrong has been committed or initiated, MBNorm is clearly, but clumsily, expressed by 'I have conscience of . . .' and MBNeg by 'I have not conscience of . . .'. This is not idiomatic of course: the obvious way of saying the former is: 'I have something on my conscience.' In the case of the latter the transference of the negative is as inevitable in English as in Greek. 'I have nothing on my conscience' is the only way to negative the verb. The difficulties are of course increased in the case of English as the substantive has always to be employed, the periphrasis with *have* being the only way of expressing the idea with a verbal phrase that will adequately convey the required connotation.

The LXX then makes 'I have nothing wrong on my conscience' the equivalent of 'my heart doth not reproach me for any of my days' (for the R.V. margin is to be preferred here). As will immediately be seen there is no ground here for supposing that the translator took *conscience* to be the translation of *heart*.

συνείδησις also occurs but once in the LXX: 'Curse not the King in thy conscience.'[3] The rendering in the R.V. is perhaps

---

[1] Cf. Socrates ap Stobaeus, *loc. cit.* (Ex 9): οἱ μηδὲν ἑαυτοῖς ἄτοπον συνειδότες . . . (ἀταράχως ζῶσιν). Possibly the translator actually had the quotation in mind while considering how to recast the passage.

[2] Cf. above, p. 26 ff and *passim*.

[3] Eccles. 10.20: ἐν συνειδήσει σου βασιλέα μὴ καταράσῃ. A.V. renders ἐν συνειδήσει αου 'in thy thought'; R.V. 'in thy heart'.

slightly to be preferred, although both are adequate. The tenor of the passage is, that however secret the *curse* may be–the knowledge of it being shared with no one at all but 'thyself'–it will be found out. Even the intimacy of private thoughts is too public for such a *curse*. Such a usage of συνείδησις is perfectly legitimate but for our present purpose it can only be classified NA.[1]

It would be a gross abuse of opportunity, now that συνείδησις is found representing a Hebrew original–even in a passage of NA connotation–not to examine that original in the hope of relating N.T. usage to a Hebrew prototype. But such a quest proves unhelpful–serving only, as does the Job passage above, to reinforce the conclusion reached from this study, that *conscience* was taken by the N.T. from Greek popular thought. For 'the Hebrew in which Ecclesiastes is written has . . . (many) . . . features . . . not met with (even) in the latest parts of the O.T. (Ezra-Nehemiah, Chronicles, Esther); but found first in fragments of Ben Sira and in the Mishnah. . . . It contains very decided admixtures of words and idioms not found before'[2]: and the word here translated συνείδησις proves to be all but a case in point. Apart from the present passage it occurs only four times in the O.T., three of these being simply repetitions of the *leitmotif* dominating a single passage. The remaining one uses the word in the same set phrase–'wisdom and understanding'–as the other three.[3] All four are in very late books, and in each case the translators render it–quite correctly in view of the contrast with σοφία–by σύνεσις.[4]

There is no other case of the use of συνείδησις in the O.T. It makes, however, two further appearances in the Apocrypha. Hopes raised by its use in Ecclesiasticus,[5] a Hebrew version of

[1] H. H. Wright's attempt in *Koheleth* to equate this passage with Rom. 13.5 and see in it an assertion that loyalty to the power is *a matter of conscience* is quite beside the point as well as being extremely tortuous.

[2] Driver: *The Language of the Old Testament*, p. 444.

[3] II Chron. 1.10, 11, 12: Solomon's prayer for *wisdom and understanding* and God's reply, and Dan. 1.17. The word is מַדָּע (*madda'*), which takes its rise from the basic יָדַע (*yada'*). This connotes 'to ascertain by seeing' and so 'to know': its similarity to the Greek Fιδ- is obvious. The same root is to be found in words meaning 'why?' or 'how?' and also 'kinswoman'. The noun *knowledge* is usually–and very commonly–represented by דַּעַת (*da'ath*); to convey another sense dependent on the same root, מַדָּע might be thought the obvious alternative.

[4] Cf. p. 19, n. 1, above.   [5] Ecclus 42.18, cited immediately below.

most of which has come to light during the past hundred years, of further light on a possible Hebrew background for the word and its idea, are due for a disappointment similar to that in the case of the Job passage.[1] It would have been as interesting, whether the view be accepted that the Hebrew version is but a retranslation from an earlier Greek text, or not, to have discovered what Hebrew word might be chosen by a translator to represent συνείδησις as to learn what Hebrew word stood in the original on which the Greek text is based. But the Greek original of 'For the most high knoweth all knowledge'[2] has no equivalent at all in the Hebrew text as found. In any case the Greek text is far from certain, and even if it be not correct to read εἴδησιν here[3] it can scarcely be doubted, in view both of the second half of the sentence[4] and of the general tenor of the passage, that συνείδησιν should be understood as but a stronger variant of εἴδησιν; that is, as NA, as in Ecclesiastes.[5]

The Wisdom occurrence, however, is more helpful. Despite a text yet again corrupt, the sense, as the Revisers comment, is clear.

> For wickedness condemned by a witness within, is a coward thing, and being pressed hard by conscience, always forecasteth the worst lot.[6]

---

[1] Job 27.6 cited above, p. 55.

[2] Ecclus 42.18 (R.V.): ἔγνω γὰρ ὁ ὕψιστος πᾶσαν συνείδησιν. Peters' attempted restoration of the deficiency is of no assistance of course, and may well be mistaken in view of what was seen in the Job passage. Nor is the attempt by the Syriac version to fill the lacuna much more helpful: for even if this be in general a translation of the original Hebrew, in many instances it corrects that text by including translations from the Greek.

[3] Following, with the Revisers, the strong testimony of Alexandrinus and Vaticanus.

[4] Ecclus 42.18[d]: καὶ ἐνέβλεψεν εἰς σημεῖον αἰῶνος.

[5] Eccles. 10.20: cited above, p. 56.

[6] Wisd. 17.11 (R.V.): reading some such text as: Δειλὸν γὰρ ἰδίως πονηρία μαρτυρεῖ καταδικαζομένη, ἀεὶ δὲ προσείληφε τὰ χαλεπὰ συνεχομένη τῇ συνειδήσει. For ἰδίως cf. Epict: Fr. 97 (Schweighaüser)–Ex 54 and 84–cited above, p. 51. Philo: *QDSI* 128 (Ex 47) cited above, p. 49, and other refs. given, p. 46, n. 2, echo the δικαστής metaphor. For the ἔνδοθεν motif here implied cf. Philo: *QDPIS* 23 (Ex 48): . . . μάρτυρος ἢ κατηγόρου λαβὼν τάξιν ἀφανῶς ἡμᾶς ἔνδοθεν ἐλέγχει–as one aspect of that element in human nature which also is ἐπιστομίζων ταῖς τοῦ συνειδότος ἡνίαις, κτλ (cf. also above, p. 41, n. 1); also Plut: *de Tranq. Anim.* 476F–477A (Ex 49) cited above, p. 47f, and Herodian IV.vii.1 (Ex 59) cited below, p. 106. For συνεχομένη cf. Vett. Val. V.i (Ex 85) in which those born with a given horoscope seem συνέχεσθαι . . . κολαζομένους κατὰ συνείδησιν as travellers κατέχονταί που by islands or deserts; *Pap. Oxy.* III 532[23] (Ex 44): ὑπὸ κακοῦ συνειδότος κατεχόμενος; and *Test. XII Patr.*; *Reub.* iv.3 (Ex 73).

Our conclusions about the Greek connotation of *conscience* could hardly ask for more complete corroboration than is here provided by the first Biblical example of its use that is not NA. *Conscience* is used absolutely. Its reference is shown by the context to be to *wickedness*. It is interpreted in terms of *condemned (from) within*, and the subject is *hard pressed* as a result, and in terror.

The attempt to trace a Hebrew original behind Wisdom has proved to be unavailing: in any case to deny the Greek background of this passage would be completely to ignore all the available evidence. For this is nothing but standard Greek MBA usage.

Before we arrive at long last at an examination of the use and meaning of *conscience* in the N.T., now that the small quantity of other Biblical appearances of the idea have been surveyed, we must notice one further relevant point. Such appearances, in any case few–of M two only for certain, making with the NA example from Ecclesiastes three altogether–are confined to the Wisdom literature, which, whether written originally in Hebrew or in Greek, represents the meeting place of the Hebrew outlook with the Greek. The assertion that the N.T., in *conscience,* 'baptised' a Greek idea is thus in no way invalidated by such earlier appearances: for these are not concerned to 'baptise' the idea. They so entirely accept it as they find it among the notions taken for granted in the Greek world, without apology or comment, that, were they not in fact 'Biblical', we should almost be obliged to include them also under the head of Greek usage. Perhaps the N.T. writers remembered reading the word in such literature: but it does not matter, for it is certain that they heard it spoken wherever they went in the Hellenistic world and always in a context and with a sense of which the remembered 'Biblical' quotations would have been no more than one or two additional examples.

VI

THE CATCHWORD OF CORINTH

The connotation of a word outside the N.T., and prior to or contemporary with it, must always be of prime significance for its understanding within the N.T. *Conscience* is one of the few important Greek words of the N.T. that have not had imported into them, through use by the LXX, a colouring from the Hebrew experience and outlook of the O.T. Our purpose so far has therefore been to arrive at as precise an estimate of the Greek connotation of this word as is possible from a close and analytical study of the wealth of evidence available in literary and popular usage.

While controversy is no part of our purpose, it is none the less puzzling to observe that, where scholars have not attempted to discover its connotation entirely by means of analysis of the internal evidence of the N.T. alone[1]–which as we shall see, uses the word without explanation or comment; they either have underestimated the amount and value of the external evidence available, or have minimised its importance.[2]

The outstanding example of this latter tendency–the assumption of a Stoic origin for the word[3]–we have already discussed at length.[4] The enquiry which arose from the rejection of that assumption, as unsupported by evidence, and inherently impro-

[1] Cf. Westcott on Heb. 9.9.

[2] Thus Lake and Cadbury's comment on Acts 23.1 (*Beginnings of Christianity*, pp. 286 ff)–among the least misleading, but still not entirely in accordance with the conclusions of this study–is cursorily dismissed by Selwyn (I *Peter*–on 3.19, p. 177) as 'not borne out by the history of the term', no other reason being advanced than Menander: *Monost*. 654 (Ex 66)–cited above, p. 41, which we saw *ibid*. to be quite inconclusive in isolation; and some Latin examples which are entirely irrelevant; together with illustrations of two other ideas whose identification with that behind συνείδησις is plain *petitio principii*.

[3] συνείδησις–as opposed perhaps to *conscientia*; cf. below, p. 118 f. For qualification of *origin* cf. pp. 13 and 15, above.

[4] Chapter I.

bable, has shown not only that it is thirdly quite unnecessary, but also that even had the Greek Stoics made frequent use of it, it would be of no importance. For the 'man-in-the-street' used it far more frequently, and its use in the N.T. 'is not to be understood as technically philosophical'.[1]

We are, then, in a position to remedy the situation if we proceed at once to apply the results of analysis of Greek usage to the N.T. occurrences as a whole. We shall classify each appearance of συνείδησις and the one instance of αὐτῷ συνειδέναι, in accordance with the category-scheme which we derived from the examination of αὐτῷ συνειδέναι, and found to be applicable, with only less precision, to the substantival equivalents of that phrase.[2] We shall then attempt to justify our analysis, *seriatim*, and concurrently with the exegesis of each passage.

If this analysis be correct several points are immediately evident. The first of these is not without force in confirming that correctness. The proportions borne one to another by the six categories are not so very different from what might have been expected as a result of our earlier analysis. The differences that exist are themselves significant. First there is not a single PTI example: it will be remembered that earlier analysis showed that while both were 'irrelevant' to a study of *conscience*, NA and PTI differed from one another not only in that the latter is confined to the technical language of philosophers; but also, and far more significantly, in that while PTI does represent substantivally the entire verbal phrase αὐτῷ συνειδέναι, NA so represents only the simple συνειδέναι. There are three NA examples in the N.T., but no PTI. Lake and Cadbury's assertion[1] is therefore entirely justified. The appearance of only two examples of MBNorm is atypical—but not so surprising if it be borne in mind that MBA is simply that variant of M that takes B for granted as the Norm. Two examples[3] have been set astride the borderline between MPG and MBNeg: the reasons for this will become clear on detailed examination of the passages. One example[4] has been placed fully on both sides of the same borderline. The content of conscience is in this case stated in two ways: MPG predomin-

---

[1] Lake and Cadbury, *loc. cit.*, p. 60, n. 2. Cf. also p. 16 f, above.
[2] See page 62.
[3] Heb. 13.18; I Pet. 3.16.   [4] II Cor. 1.12.

OCCURRENCES OF *CONSCIENCE* IN THE NEW TESTAMENT ANALYSED

CLASSIFICATION	PAUL		PAULINE A		PAULINE B	I Pet.	(John)
	Cor.	Rom.	Pastorals	Acts	Hebrews		
NA[7]	II.4.2 II.5.11					2.19	
MPG	II.1.12						
MB — Neg	(II.1.12)				13.18[5]	3.16[3]	
	I.4.4[1]		I Tim. 1.5[3]	23.1[3]	10.2	3.21[3]	
			I Tim. 1.19[3]	24.16[6]			
			I Tim. 3.9[4]				
			II Tim. 1.3[4]				
MB — Norm					10.22 9.14		
MB — A—	I.8.7	2.15	I Tim. 4.2		9.9		8.9
	I.8.10	9.1	Tit.1.15				
	I.8.12	13.5[2]					
	I.10.25[2]						
	I.10.27[2]						
	I.10.28[2]						
	I.10.29*						

* συνείδησις occurs twice in I Cor. 10.29.

[1] I Cor. 4.4 is the sole N.T. instance of αὐτῷ συνειδέναι.
[2] The phrase διὰ τὴν συνείδησιν—rendered by AV *for conscience sake.*
[3] Epithet ἀγαθὴ applied to συνείδησις.
[4] Epithet καθαρά applied to συνείδησις.
[5] Epithet καλή applied to συνείδησις.
[6] Epithet ἀπρόσκοπος applied to συνείδησις.
[7] NA, of course, as will be shown, cannot properly be rendered *conscience* at all.

ates, but the MBNeg element although minor, is still definite. St. Paul, it will be seen, asserts the positive in denial of a charge made against him.

Thus, in all, the N.T. presents three cases of NA–two Pauline, both from II Corinthians, and one Petrine; one and two 'halves' MPG, one Pauline, one of the 'halves' 'Pauline B', and the other Petrine. The remaining twenty-seven and two '$\frac{1}{2}$ cases' are all MB. Of these no less than thirteen are Pauline, and eight of them, perhaps even nine–it will be shown–in the context of a single controversy with one local church. A further eight are Pauline A; four and one half Pauline B and the remaining two and a half non-Pauline. Not only therefore is St. Paul the first to employ the idea of *conscience* in the N.T.; he is also so much its most frequent user that those others who use it are mainly writers who are concerned, with the best of motives, to claim Pauline authority for what they write. Pauline use is, therefore, normative for the N.T. and has at least a strong claim to be normative for Christianity as a whole.

The subdivisions 'Paul', 'Pauline A' and 'B', speak for themselves. It is not within the scope of this study to engage in questions of authorship. The Corinthian and Roman epistles are generally accepted as by Paul himself, but a strong body of competent opinion denies his authorship of the Pastorals. If these last be a pseudepigraph then they can justly be grouped with those speeches of Paul recorded in *oratio recta* by the author of Acts. Hebrews is not a pseudepigraph: it is a deliberately anonymous piece of writing, nowhere claiming Pauline authorship for itself. Nevertheless the ascription of it to St. Paul is sufficiently early in the tradition for it to be included here as 'Pauline'–albeit 'B'. If the appearances of *conscience* within these works may be taken as evidence of authentic reminiscence, particularly in the case of the speeches from Acts, it is equally effective as evidence of conscious, but bad, imitation. Our analysis[1] might well serve as additional ammunition against a theory of Pauline authorship, the usage being so noticeably inclined towards MBNeg–as opposed to the dominant MBA of the undisputedly Pauline epistles. The only MBNegs in St. Paul are: (*a*) what is little more than a corollary of an MPG, and (*b*) a use of the verbal phrase. The

[1] p. 62.

masterly use of συνείδησις in Hebrews, integrated with the sweeping crescendo of the theme, as will be seen later,[1] militates equally strongly against the theory of a Hebrew original.

The case in a few texts of the *Pericope de Adultera*[2] is of particular interest as being a summing up from outside the N.T. of the N.T. doctrine of the conscience. It is to be noted that it can only be classified MBA.

St. Paul in his undisputed epistles refers to conscience only in the two *Corinthian* letters and in that to the Romans. While the references in Romans are well spaced those in I Corinthians with one exception[3] occur in two 'lumps', both of which are concerned with the one subject–meat sacrificed to idols. The tone of both passages is that of rebuke. Indeed the whole of I Corinthians is hardly less severe than that of the 'severe letter' itself. St. Paul's motive in writing is to try to put an end to the disputes that bid fair to destroy his work at Corinth. He starts to work as soon as the introductory paragraph is over[4]: he feels he cannot do all that has to be done by letter only[5] but even after writing this verse he is constrained to continue his attempt at a preliminary correction of error. Sufficient clues are given in his words whereby an idea may be gained of the sort of problems with which he was faced; some of them at least may be described as *gentile presuppositions*, with which he has not hitherto met. Sometimes gently, sometimes sternly, never without a hint of irony, he grants these presuppositions for the sake of argument, and then still shows his readers to have erred. Not to stray from the matter in hand in order to produce examples of this in general, it must be said at once that there is every indication that among these *presuppositions* there stands that which can be summed up in the catch-word *conscience*.

Up till now in his ministry, so far as his surviving writings, or, for what it is worth, the author of Acts, attest, he has not used the word. It is now forced on him by the exigences of his ministry. This is most clearly seen in the passage[6] in which St. Paul sets up the claims of the controversialists, putting them in their mouths in an imaginary dialogue, and then showing how they are insufficient as guides for conduct. That which is fitting;

---

[1] Chapter XI.   [2] John 8.9.   [3] I Cor. 4.4.
[4] I Cor. 1.10 ff.   [5] I Cor. 11.34.   [6] I Cor. 10.23 ff.

edification; seeking the good of others; faith; hope; love; all these have to be taken into account. 'This *conscience*', he says, 'that you keep throwing in my face–I grant you that it has its uses. It's no good, however, telling me your conscience is clear. Mine is clear too but that is not enough–"yet am I not hereby justified".'[1] This is the first recorded occasion in Christian history–but very far from the last–when disruptive tendencies within the Church have made a battle-cry of *conscience*.

But if this explains why St. Paul first uses *conscience* in I Corinthians it is still not making clear precisely what it meant to him. The relation between Galatians and Romans offers one case of St. Paul forced, in the battle to save a Church from its own errors, to rush violently into a new field of doctrine, but later, the battle being won, consolidating his gains, and systematising, in a fashion as nearly consistent as possible, the truths that controversy has forced him to maintain. A comparison of I Cor. 8.7 ff, and 10.23 ff with Romans 14–in both of which *the weak brother*[2] is the central character and his preservation from *occasion of stumbling*[3] in matters of food and drink the object–offers not insufficient justification for seeing a similar relation between I Corinthians and Romans. What Romans is to Galatians in the case of justification, the Law, faith and works, it is also to I Corinthians in the case, at least, of *conscience*. Although, therefore, the use in I Corinthians is the earlier it is best approached by way of that in Romans, as representing the fruit of St. Paul's mature and calmer deliberation.

---

[1] I Cor. 4.4 (R.V.): οὐδὲν γὰρ ἐμαυτῷ σύνοιδα, ἀλλ' οὐκ ἐν τούτῳ δεδικαίωμαι.
[2] ὁ ἀσθενής.   [3] πρόσκομμα.

E

VII

CONSCIENCE AND WRATH

THE first significant point revealed by a consideration of Romans in the context of *meats* is an added confirmation of what is indicated above, and is indeed obvious enough; that is, that while St. Paul was willing to grant the word *conscience* to the Corinthians if they wished to use it, he himself was not impressed by it, considering it neither of great importance in itself, nor, particularly, of any great help in the matter of *meats*. For when he comes, without heat, and without prior knowledge of the views prevalent in the Church to which he is writing, to discuss the same matter,[1] he does not hint at, let alone mention, *conscience* at all, while in practically all other details he duplicates or develops the 'Corinthian ruling'. The inference is irresistible, that *conscience* was introduced into Christianity under pressure from Corinth, as bound up with a controversial issue.

At the same time St. Paul never ran away from difficulties. 'Romans is the finished product . . . the earlier epistles' [having given] 'glimpses of the workshop in which St. Paul's thought was hammered out'.[2] Into it 'he has packed . . . the fruits of many years of thought and work, of preaching, controversy and the cure of souls'.[3] He may not have liked very much the idea of *conscience*–at best, as will be seen, a negative thing and a *pis aller* –but the Corinthian controversialists had forced it upon his notice, nor could he deny that it was, as we already have clearly seen, a real experience, familiar to and understood by the Gentile world. He recognised a duty to find a place for it in his comprehensive scheme, particularly in that epistle that most roundly asserts that the Gentile world's experience was valid so far as it went.

[1] Rom. 14.
[2] Dodd: *The Epistle of Paul to the Romans*, p. xxx.
[3] *Ibid.*, p. xxv f.

66

In the fulfilment of this duty he still places only a minor value on *conscience* and refers to it only three times.[1] Nevertheless in so doing he has extracted the marrow of the matter from Gentile experience and has incorporated it with fairness into his total scheme. The passage in which the meaning he assigns to it is most clearly revealed by the context, and which must therefore be normative not only for Romans, nor even for the Pauline writings, but for the N.T. as a whole, is Romans 13.5.

Herein he discusses the duty of the Christian to the secular government. He claims that there is 'no power but of God' and that 'the powers that be are (therefore) ordained of God'.[2] They are to be obeyed in fear because they 'bear not the sword in vain'.[3] They have, in fact, authority from God to punish, in order to maintain that civil order which is a reflection, however imperfect, of the Divine order. Thus they can be described as, within their own field, the mediators of *the Wrath*. The definition of this latter concept as *the principle of retribution inherent in a moral universe*[4] and as *impersonal*[5] is in some ways adequate, but finally unsatisfying in that it does violence to the Biblical experience of God on the one hand, and on the other cannot be consistently maintained. It takes its rise from the natural reluctance, particularly of the Christian, to attribute to God *the irrational passion of anger*.[6] But it is not a little question-begging to define *anger* as a *passion* and, having done so, to go on to call it *irrational*. The Jew thought of God primarily, as also of human morals, in terms not of dispositions and attitudes, but of acts. That the two cannot be entirely separated is true, but even on the human level the rejection of unworthy material, or the beating of the misshapen into shape, can be accomplished without passion, and could be not unjustly regarded as a completely rational act. Again, on the human level, it is the forces that tend to mitigate the cold rationality of such action that are more truly of the nature of passion, that is, regret of the necessity of the action, and the love, of the object acted upon, from which it springs. But, in any case, if *the Wrath* is to be thought of as *an inevitable process of cause and effect in a moral universe*,[7] there is no escape from the twin corollaries; first, that *cause and effect* is an inferred law, part of the order

---

[1] Rom. 2.15, 9.1, 13.5. [2] Rom. 13.1. [3] Rom. 13.4.
[4] Dodd, *op. cit.*, p. 204. [5] *Ibid.*, pp. 21 and 24. [6] *Ibid.*, p. 24. [7] *Ibid.*, p. 23.

of things as they are, and therefore, on theistic, and particularly the Jewish, premises, directly ordained and controlled by God; and second, that if the universe be in fact moral, it is only so as the creation of God, who has made it in a certain way, and maintains constant oversight of it to his own good ends. That the Biblical writers in their witness faced squarely the most dangerous implications of this could be shown by instances embarrassing in their richness: to avoid straying too far from our present course, the two most fearless statements only need be cited. The prophet, whether or not he is thinking specifically of the Persian *Ormuzd-Ahriman* dualism, certainly rejects all dualism–including that of *Personal God–Impersonal Universe* (or *Law*)–when he hears God say: 'I form the light and create darkness; I make peace and create evil; I am the Lord, that doeth all these things'.[1] Herein he goes not a whit further than his predecessor's 'Can a bird fall in a snare upon the earth, where no gin is set for him? . . . shall the trumpet be blown in a city, and the people not be afraid? shall evil befall a city, and the Lord hath not done it?'[2] If it is desirable to avoid crude anthropomorphism, it is possible never, like St. Paul, to use the verb *to be angry* with God as subject: but it is hardly possible, particularly for a Jew, to deny that *the Wrath* is *of God*. That St. Paul remained a Jew in this matter as in so many others, the present passage is a sufficient indication. The civil power, when it operates as an *avenger for Wrath to him that doeth evil*,[3] does so in its capacity of a *minister of God*.[4]

St. Paul, then, conceives of the Universe as the creation and realm of the personal God, who is the Father of our Lord Jesus Christ. But that creation and its government are orderly. Each element of which it is composed has its due place, function and nature: that the delicate balance may be maintained each has certain fixed and unalterable limits.[5] Should such limits be transgressed, the order of things reacts by the sequence of cause and effect to rectify the wrong.[6] The purpose of such limits is not penal, but beneficent. Within them there is joy: but were

---

[1] Isa. 45.7. [2] Amos 3.5f. [3] Rom. 13.4. [4] *Ibid.*
[5] Cf. Job 38.10 ff; Ps. 148.6; Acts 17.26, etc.
[6] This is not unlike the great Greek conception of Justice; cf. the classic exposition in Anaximander, cited Simplicius; *Phys* xxiv.13. That, however, is hardly to its detriment.

they to be transgressed with impunity the Divine order would dissolve into chaos.[1] Thus this reaction of the order of things against the transgressor is painful to him, and may be regarded as penal: this is *the Wrath* falling upon those elements of the creation that overstep the limits within which they were created 'to live and move and have their being'.[2]

But man is himself an element of the creation. His nature is in all ways subject to beneficent limitation, both externally as to place–he cannot live under water, and will fall to the ground unless supported, being heavier than air: and internally as to function–a too high sugar content in his blood will kill him as surely as a too low, and his flesh will blister if he place his feet in the fire. This distinction cannot be pressed very far: the point is that man, being what he is in himself and as a part of the created order, is subject to essential limitations which he transgresses only at his peril.

He is thus subject to three pressures, complementary and overlapping but nevertheless distinguishable. There is the pressure of his place in creation as a whole, and there is that of his place in the society of men.[3] These pressures are exerted, almost literally, to 'keep him in his place'–but they are, none the less, beneficent, because it is only in his place that he belongs, can 'feel at home', be a happy man. Out of 'his place' he would only be 'like a fish out of water'. Nevertheless if he should resist these pressures, try to leave 'his place' and transcend the limits within which he is created and ordained by God to live, he will suffer: in the case of the first pressure, natural calamity, so rightly called in legal parlance *Act of God*, for it is *the Wrath* mediated by nature as opposed to human institutions: in the case of the second pressure *the Sword*–if such a term be very widely interpreted to include all the shades of penalty, from death by torture to unpopularity, that the various types of human institution or society can inflict: this is *the Wrath* mediated by human society. They can be referred to in one word as *the Wrath*, and

---

[1] Cf. Gen. 1.2.   [2] Acts 17.28.

[3] The tensions between the pressures exerted by the varied types of society (e.g. Family; labour-unit; nation; Church; apart from the other more or less voluntary associations for specific purposes) within society as such (i.e. mankind as a whole) must be ignored here. But cf. Brunner: *The Divine Imperative* particularly Cap. XXX and its detailed discussion in Bk. III, Secs. II ff.

they are part of a beneficent order of things-as-they-are, that is, of God's order.

But nothing has so far been said of the third pressure, no less beneficent but more ineluctable, for it is nearer home, being that of the man's own internal constitution and nature. Being integrally involved with the nature of the universe as a whole, and with that of society and societies, it applies its pressure, often at least, in co-operation with and as complementary to that of the external world. When this pressure is resisted, the internal nature of man reacts against that resistance. To eat is natural to man: if he overeat, or starve, that is, if he transgress the limits of his nature as an eater, he will fall sick. If he eat arsenic, an unnatural thing to eat, the resulting sickness is an instance of the co-operation and complementary action of this internal *Wrath* with the external. Only, however, if the notion be accepted that what is contrary to nature is, thereby, *morally* wrong[1] can the operation of *the Wrath* be regarded as exclusively moral. Nevertheless, as inherent in Man's nature are also *moral* limitations,[2] it will have a moral aspect. If *the moral* be regarded as necessarily including the element of choice in its connotation, then indigestion or poisoning are not simply an analogy of, but are truly a reaction of man's internal nature parallel to, that reaction of it against the immoral, the wrong act (with its implied disposition or character) which is *conscience*. Man by his nature and as an element both in society and in creation as a whole is liable to suffer, should he rebel against the limitations thereby involved, *the Wrath*, either external, or internal, or both. When the rebellion takes the form of a moral wrong, that internal *Wrath* is what St. Paul understands by *conscience*.

While the nature of creation as a whole is relatively straightforward and reliable, that of human society, partly because of the tensions between societies within it, and between any or all of them and society as such, and partly because man is *from his birth prone to sin*,[3] can be bewildering and unstable. As a result it is possible for the same act to be natural and morally right in itself–

---

[1] As it was, for example, by Stoicism.

[2] Whether these also apply to any extent to any other members of the creation is not relevant at this stage: the Bible certainly regards them as applying to man, and the Greek world from which it adopted *conscience* did not materially disagree.

[3] *Book of Common Prayer* (1928). Office for Public Baptism of Infants.

that is not liable to *the Wrath* which is natural calamity, nor to *the Wrath* which is *conscience*–while being against the law of one or other of the societies in which he who acted is involved. But as he is involved he owes loyalty,[1] and must accept the punishment he receives as just, that is to say as *the Wrath* mediated by a human society, which, according to St. Paul, has authority from God to inflict such punishment, as *the minister of God*.[2]

The meaning therefore of Romans 13.5 is 'It is your duty to God to be subject to the power: to rebel is not only illegal therefore: it is also morally wrong. It is not simply punishment by society that awaits the rebel, and the fear of which should deter him: it is also, for the law can be broken on occasion with impunity, the more terrible and less avoidable–for it is within him–pain of conscience. And both are parallel manifestations of God in action to maintain the order of things: the one is *the Wrath* external and mediated by society, the other is its internal counterpart.'

This sketch of that element of St. Paul's doctrine which includes his view of the State, and its authority, and that of other societies, is plainly inadequate in itself.[3] It is however adequate for our present purpose, that of sufficiently setting the stage on which the Pauline *conscience* must be seen to be understood. Against such a background its meaning is obvious: it is the pain a man suffers when he has done wrong. It is of the nature of things as they are that he should so suffer. Various interpretations have been offered of this particular passage, doing more or less justice to it in isolation. But we have to find an interpretation

---

[1] Cf. the classic expression in Plato's *Crito*.   [2] Rom. 13.4.

[3] It is inadequate even if the one or two qualifying considerations touched upon here be given their full weight. At the same time, however, I am far from convinced that it will not prove to be the necessary starting-point, however much qualified, mitigated and adapted, for any adequately balanced doctrine of the State or of any organised society within it (cf. again, Brunner, *loc. cit.*). Still less am I convinced that our outline is not a fair representation of nearly all that St. Paul has to say on the subject, at least in his surviving writings. Before we too hastily condemn this giving *carte blanche* to human government as Divinely ordained as impossibly naif, we should remember that it was written in the full awareness of the author that the two main societies to which he owed allegiance by birth had combined to crucify his Lord not long before: and that he himself had suffered cruelly at the hands of the one and ran the risk of death from the other more and more every day. Although he appealed to Rome for protection from the Jews, we do him less than justice if we suppose his view of the State to be coloured mainly by an illusory estimate of the worth of this particular example, rather than by a deep theological insight.

that will not only make sense of the remaining N.T. occurrences as well as this one, but will also bear a reasonable relation to the non-Biblical usage of the word of which we have examined ample evidence. The word is used absolutely–but in a stylistic construction that indicates its being parallel to *the Wrath*–and in a context plainly concerned with the wrongness or otherwise of acts. This study has already shown that MA is always MBA, and the parallelism with *the Wrath* only serves to confirm and illuminate this conclusion. St. Paul takes the Greek idea and sets it firmly and brilliantly in a significant but hardly, as will be seen, pre-eminent place in his Judaeo-Christian *Weltanschauung*.

While at this stage such an assertion is all but self-evidently true, and almost any MB example would serve to support it, a Thyatiran tombstone inscription is perhaps the most interesting. It is set up by a man '. . . to his own wife. No one else shall be authorised to lay anyone to rest here, nor to take the tomb for another, nor to deface the inscription. Should anyone act contrary to these provisions, may he lie under the wrath of God, who judges living and dead, and his own conscience: he shall in addition be liable to be fined by the city of Thyatira.'[1] The close parallel afforded by this with Rom. 13.5 needs little emphasis. *Conscience* is used absolutely but its reference is made clear: *his own* indicates that it is the result of the wrongdoers own act, and the context shows that it would be a bad act. Parallel with it is both the notion of the *Wrath of God*–the Greek says *God enraged* using for *enraged* a word other than St. Paul's *orge*–and that of the power of the State to inflict temporal penalties.

No form of writing that survives–not even private correspondence–partakes more certainly of the commonplace and popular than tombstone inscriptions: the ideas expressed in them are invariably platitudes–for it is with the platitude–the formal expression of *volkspsyche*–that man outfaces the great and universal issues that confront him–and none is more universal than death. Whenever this inscription may be dated,[2] the appearance of

---

[1] *Ath. Mitt.* xxiv.237 (Ex 89)=*C.I.G.* II.3518; but Humann and Conze decipher more in the former, giving the text: . . . τῇ ἑαυτοῦ γυναικί. ἑτέρῳ δὲ οὐδενὶ ἐξέσται θεῖναί τινα, οὐδὲ ἐξαλλοτριῶσαι, οὐδὲ τὴν ἐπιγραφὴν ἐκκόψαι· εἰ δέ τις ἐναντίον ποιήσει τούτων, τὸν κρίνοντα ζῶντας καὶ νεκροὺς Θεὸν κεχολωμένον ἔχοιτο, καὶ τὴν ἰδίαν συνείδησιν· καὶ ὑποκείσεται τῇ Θυατειρηνῶν πόλει προστείμῳ.

[2] No date is attempted by the scholars who record the inscription. I incline to a date later than the N.T. and suppose this in fact to be a Christian grave. My main

conscience so used in it is the strongest confirmation of our conclusions as to the meaning not only of Rom. 13.5 but also of the
Greek *conscience* in general. This particular inscription seems,
however, to be but a variant form of a standardised and con-
ventional curse on tomb-desecrators. The variations are more-
over just such as might have been expected from a Christian,
conscious of the contrast between the pagan attitude to potential
enemies and that required of him by his faith. The pagan curse[1]
begins with 'No one else shall be authorised . . .' and with some
minor differences of detail in the middle, closes with '. . . nor to
deface the inscription'; after this however it goes on to threaten
any who would ignore this declaration in the words 'may he
perish utterly with his children and all his kin'. The Thyatiran
alteration of this conclusion seems to echo a Christian outlook
in its precise form as much as in its general tone. Instead of
calling down a specific vengeance on the desecrators it appears
deliberately to *give place unto wrath*,[2] and deliver them to the
judgment of the *Lord of both the dead and the living*.[3] The bathetic
reference to the civil penalty, and the confidence that *conscience*
will sufficiently punish the wrongdoer, complete a parallel to
Rom. 13.5 which is so marked that it is hard not to see some
relation, mediate or immediate, between them. The date of the
inscription is thus not of vital significance for if it be regarded
as so worded under Christian influence, and in the Christian era,

reason will be made clear in the text from a comparison of this inscription with
that recorded at *C.I.G.* II.2831 (cf. below, n. 1). Neither its location in the Ar-
menian cemetery at Thyatira, the use of an inscribed tombstone, nor the attribution
to a (singular) God of judgeship over living and dead are decisive in isolation,
however suggestive in combination with each other and with the more positive
factors. Neither communal burying places nor inscribed stones are peculiar to nor
originated by Christianity. Nor was it the notion of God judging that was ludicrous
to the Greek world, but only that of his doing so by the agency of *a man raised from
the dead* (Acts 17.31 f). But Thyatira did of course see the very early foundation of
a Christian Church of some importance (Rev. 2.18 ff) and a third of its population
still professes Christianity despite the many vicissitudes that have changed it into
Ak-Hissar.

[1] *C.I.G.* II.2831.   [2] Rom. 12.19–but using χολόω instead of ὀργίζω.
[3] Rom. 14.9–if these two verses are so alluded to they are only twenty-five
verses apart. Possibly the whole passage was in the husband's mind when he commissioned the inscription: perhaps even he had recently heard it read–and expounded
–in Church. This would account for the extraordinarily close parallel with Rom.
13.5 which of course is the centre of the passage. Perhaps also in his mind was the
Nicene formula κρῖναι ζῶντας καὶ νεκρούς: this need not imply a post-Nicene date
as the same phrase occurs in the symbol, on which Nicaea based its own, offered
by Eusebius as long used in his Church in catechising and as a baptismal confession.

it is relevant to point out that despite such influence *conscience* still remains what this study has shown it consistently to have been in pagan use in such a context. If a pre-Christian date, or no Christian influence be posited, then it is a further example of MBA usage of particular significance as entirely supporting our reading of this passage.[1]

Before we close this chapter we must notice St. Paul's carefully emphatic use of 'Ἀνάγκη here. The English versions' possible but very weak rendering *ye must needs* does not, we may feel with some certainty, begin to do justice to it in this context. Its meaning and its ready adaptability to a Christian scheme are obvious, as we saw when we discussed its occurrence in connection with *conscience* in Greek writers.[2] No Greek contemporary of St. Paul–indeed few modern commentators–could avoid, in connection with *conscience* and *the Wrath*, thinking of such figures as the Eumenides[3] and Nemesis.[4] 'Ἀνάγκη has the advantages of (*a*) belonging to the same group of ideas as these two; (*b*) being more comprehensive in scope than both put together; (*c*) being abstract, and (*d*) being patient of use with ἐστί followed by the infinitive. If the Pagan reader would have taken the passage to mean 'It is of the fixed nature of things (including man and society) as they are to be subject', the Christian, even had St. Paul not explicitly affirmed that *there is no power but of God*,[5] would have no doubt as to the meaning. 'It is the sovereign will of God that ye should be in subjection: if ye disobey God's will in this ye therefore do so at your peril–pains await you if ye do; if not the external pains of civil punishment, at any rate the internal pains that men call conscience.'

---

[1] Cf. also Isoc: *to Demonicus* 16 (Ex 27): μηδέποτε μηδὲν αἰσχρὸν ποιήσας ἔλπιζε λήσειν· καὶ γὰρ ἂν τοὺς ἄλλους λάθῃς, σεαυτῷ συνειδήσεις–which brings into relation the external and internal consequences of the shameful act. Also Vett. Val. V.i (Ex 85), cited above, p. 58. The principle set out in Epict: Fr. 97 (Schweighaüser) (Ex 54 and 84), cited above, p. 51 could hardly ask for a better concrete illustration.

[2] Cf. above, p. 40 ff and notes.

[3] Diodorus Siculus iv.65 (Ex 78) adapts the legend of Amphiaraos–one of the Seven against Thebes. He, undertaking this ill-fated expedition under the goad of his wife Eriphyle, who had been bribed with Harmonia's necklace, nevertheless charged his children, in the sure event of his death which as a seer he foreknew, to kill their mother in revenge. Alcmaeon his son obeyed the charge and, the legend said, was driven mad by the Eumenides. Diodorus modernises this with διὰ τὴν συνείδησιν τοῦ μύσους εἰς μανίαν περιέστη; cf. also *Or*. 395 f (Ex 17 and 56), cited above, p. 47, where Euripides treats the Orestes legend in the same way.

[4] Cf. Dodd, *op. cit.*, p. 29.   [5] Rom. 13.1., Cf. John 19.11.

VIII

CONSCIENCE AND THE
WEAK BROTHER

FROM the passage just considered it is convenient to go straight
to I Cor. 10 as three of the five occurrences in this latter passage
occur in the phrase *for conscience sake*[1] which also occurs in the
former. The natural interpretation of the first two occurrences,[2]
that is, *because of conscience avoid asking questions* is authenticated
here in three ways. First, the tendencious interpretation *do not
let your conscience force you to ask questions* would only be unequivocally expressed by a different order of the words.[3] This weights
probability very strongly in favour of the natural interpretation,
but is not in itself decisive. Added to the other two it is overwhelming. Second: if 10.25, 27 are to be so taken then 10.28
must be so taken also, the result being, absurdly, *do not let your
informant and your conscience force you to eat*; whereas the only possible
interpretation in the context is *you must not eat, for two reasons*:
(*a*) *the avoidance of occasion of stumbling*[4] *to the informant*, and (b)
conscience. St. Paul goes on, it is true, to forestall the controversialists' claim that there would be no conscience about it
because they knew better, to say that these two reasons are by
way of a hendiadys; but this is an afterthought, which as v. 29
shows raises a fresh difficulty that he has to deal with by the
dialogue method—but more about that later. Even if the hendiadys be taken as his first intention, *do not let your informant's
conscience force you to eat* is still absurd as the context demands
the exact opposite—*let your informant's conscience compel you not to eat*.
Third, the natural interpretation is the one supported by the other
use of the same phrase, in Rom. 13.5.

The meaning of the phrase is perhaps most aptly illustrated by

[1] διὰ τὴν συνείδησιν.
[3] I.e. μηδὲν διὰ τὴν συνείδησιν ἀνακρίνοντες.
[2] I Cor. 10.25 and 27.
[4] πρόσκομμα.

the English proverb: 'What you don't know won't hurt you.' The Christian who discovered that what he was eating was in effect a share in the *table of devils* should, according to the preceding paragraph,[1] in St. Paul's view, be assailed by the pain of conscience. To meat in itself there could be no objection–'The earth is the Lord's and the fulness thereof'[2]–and the Christian could partake, giving God thanks.[3] But sacrificial meats were in a different category–although God's in origin they had been by sacrifice (mis)appropriated to Demons, and become a means of communion with them. But, although much if not most of the meat eaten in the Pagan environment was made available by sacrificial slaughter, there was no means of identifying it definitely as such in the shop or on the table except by deliberate enquiry. 'Eat it and ask no questions', says St. Paul. 'If you were to discover that it was *idol-meat*, after you had eaten it, then you would suffer conscience.'

There are two points of significance in this passage. The first, remarked upon by almost all commentators, is that St. Paul makes no appeal to the Jerusalem decree.[4] This is strong support for the present contention, that *conscience* was the 'battle-cry' of the Corinthian trouble-makers. It is clear that *conscience* only came into its own in the Greek world after the collapse of the city-state. The close integration of politics with ethics, with the former predominant, was no longer possible: there was no sufficiently close authority, external to the individual, effectively to direct conduct. Consequently, as a *pis aller*, men fell back on the internal chastisement of *conscience* as the only authority. So too, as this epistle clearly shows, and the 'severe letter' underlines, in the Corinthian Church external authority was in dispute and, thence, in disrepute; and, once again, its members fell back on *conscience*. St. Paul, therefore, recognises that it is useless to appeal to any pronouncement of authority. He had probably laid down the Jerusalem regulations at the outset of his Corinthian ministry: the present trouble would then have arisen partly from the Corinthians' defiance of them in the name of *gnosis*. The Corinthians were, after all, fornicating[5] as well as eating idol-meats.

---

[1] I Cor. 10.14-22. [2] *Ibid.*, v.26 citing Ps. 24.1.
[3] Cf. with I Cor. 10.30, Rom. 14.6.
[4] Acts 15.29. [5] I Cor. 5.1 ff.

But in any case St. Paul prefers to meet his flock on ground of their own choosing.

The second significant thing is that here conscience is to some extent regarded as dependent on an assessment on other grounds of the quality of acts. In this case it is knowledge of the source of the meat eaten that brings on the pain, not the eating of the meat. Even in its negative and limited function, conscience does not so much indicate that an act committed is wrong, as that an act 'known' (by other means, and rightly or wrongly) to be wrong, has been committed. This, as will be seen, is even more clearly demonstrated in the earlier Corinthians[1] passage.

In the Romans passage[2] St. Paul mitigates this judgment very considerably–conscience is an objectively real pressure of a man's internal nature against rebellion–but he does not entirely reverse it: for he is at pains to supply the Roman Christians with the knowledge, on other grounds, that such rebellion is wrong. Doubtless this, in common with the others, is an element of conscience that he accepted as he found it at Corinth. It was certainly an essential part of his opponents' argument, as will appear from examination of I Cor. 8.

Before that, however, consideration must be completed of I Cor. 10. The keynote of the passage, as has been seen, St. Paul allows the controversialists to set. *All things are lawful*[3] is twice[4] put into their mouths to be refuted; later a third comment[5] is also put into their mouths, and all three tend in the same direction. Some at least of the Corinthians were claiming, according to St. Paul, that they had *gnosis*[6] and that, therefore, they could eat meat, even if known to be *sacrificial*, with no painful consequences. If others were so ignorant as to be assailed by conscience after so morally neutral an act as eating meat, that was their look-out. 'Oh no', replies St. Paul, 'eating meat, as you and I well know, is morally neutral, certainly; but refusal of responsibility for others is morally disgraceful.' The Christian is to be guided by positive considerations, not negative. The right question is not 'Is it harmless?'[3] but 'Is it beneficial?'[7] and 'Does it build up the Body, the Brotherhood, in which we are all members one of another,

---

[1] I Cor. 8.7 ff., see below p. 79 ff.   [2] Rom. 13.5, see above, p. 67 ff.
[3] πάντα ἔξεστιν.   [4] I Cor. 10.23.   [5] *Ibid.*, v.30   [6] *Ibid.*, v. 8.1.
[7] Cf. οὐ πάντα συμφέρει, *ibid.*

and in which all are hurt by the hurt of one?'[1] Vv. 24 and 33 sum up the decisive principle. The answer, therefore, to the question 'Why is my liberty judged of another's conscience?'[2]–a question put into the controversialists' mouths by St. Paul–is that it is a duty incumbent on love to protect the brother from the pain of conscience. *Conscience* in this question is of course the same here as elsewhere in this passage: it is the pain consequent upon committing the (supposedly) wrong act, into which the *little one* has been led by the example of his more *knowledgeable* brother.

Such an interpretation is in any case required by the passage but it is borne out not only by the occurrences in I Cor. 8 but also by that in I Cor. 4.4, wherein the notion of any man's conscience adequately judging himself, let alone another, is emphatically and scornfully rejected by St. Paul. It is not the *weak brother's* views that restrain an unwilling brother from the eating he knows to be harmless, but the desire, springing from love, to spare him pain, and to 'give no occasion of stumbling either to Jews or Greeks or to the Church of God'.[3]

The last occurrence of *conscience* in this passage[4] needs no comment–it is simply the repetition of the occurrence immediately preceding in order to give it a new twist by way of afterthought. St. Paul did not wish to lose half his converts by forbidding them meat: but at the same time he really disapproved of the eating of sacrificial meats[5]: were he to discover he had eaten them he would himself suffer conscience. He writes vv. 23-28 solving the problem for himself–but in v. 28 he remembers that the issue is precisely that those whom he addresses are claiming that even if they knew from the start that the meats were sacrificial, they would still have no conscience about it: he therefore makes this rapid twist, and by the piece of additional dialogue examined above solves the further difficulty it raises. In any case the meaning of *conscience* remains constant throughout the passage.

Rom. 14 will not be examined, as the meaning of *conscience* is the sole present concern. It is nevertheless of great value that it

---

[1] Cf. οὐ πάντα οἰκοδομεῖ, *ibid.*   [2] I Cor. 10.29
[3] I Cor. 10.32: for ἀπρόσκοπος, see below, p. 95, n. 3.
[4] *Ibid.*, v.29.   [5] Cf. *ibid.* vv. 14 ff.

exists. For the argument in I Corinthians is very much not only *ad hominem* but also *ad hoc*: its form is so much dictated by the situation at, and the catchwords of, Corinth, that what St. Paul really intends might remain obscure were the more considered statement not available. The confusion of approach is nowhere more manifest than in this matter of idol meats, in that I Cor. 10.23 ff is little more than a recovering of the ground of I Cor. 8. The later passage however is gentler in tone and concedes more to the Corinthians. I Cor. 8 is so withering that St. Paul doubtless felt it necessary later to mitigate his tone very considerably. 'So you know all the answers, do you? Well let me tell you that *knowledge* by itself just fills you full of hot air; it is love that builds, and builds solidly. Really worthwhile knowledge–which it is quite obvious you have not yet achieved–springs from loving God'[1]: 'A fine way to use your Christian freedom, to set a stumbling block before *the weak.*'[2]

It is within such a mood and context that the meaning of *conscience* must be sought: there are two necessary preliminaries to the search. Firstly there is the textual problem in v. 7. Critics in general seem to be agreed that συνηθεία should be read here.[3] While it would not be impossible to interpret the passage reading συνειδήσει–yet in this case it would be necessary to classify it as NA. Its use then in close proximity to three MBA occurrences, serving as one of the two foci of a controversial passage, would be very surprising.

The second question is: Who are *the Weak*? The appearance in this passage, as well as in 10.23 ff and Rom. 14, of the *occasion of stumbling* motif, relates it at once to such teaching as that in Luke 17.1 f (=Matt. 18.6). Whether or not Mark 9.42 is the source of the former two, there is no reason to doubt that all three represent an authentic saying of Our Lord. Matthew however incorporates it, together with other material including some peculiar to himself, in such a way as to produce what is virtually an essay on ecclesiastical discipline,[4] in which the two normative

---

[1] Cf. I Cor. 8.1-3.   [2] Cf. *ibid.*, vv. 9.11.

[3] The great Greek Uncials strongly support this view, while the Latin influence in the MSS. and Versions that read συνειδήσει is predominant. *Conscientia* in Latin is a possible rendering of what is conveyed by συνηθεία–that is, the getting used to an idea by familiarity with it. It is, further, easy to see how, in a passage reiterating the συνείδησις refrain, copyists might have added one more.

[4] Two of the only three gospel occurrences of ἐκκλησία are in this chapter.

themes are forgiveness of others and avoidance of *occasion of stumbling* to the *little ones*.

While it is perhaps not always easy to accept the arguments of Thornton[1] yet there can be little doubt that he is right in his contention that *the weak* are the same people as *the little ones*, those to whom St. Paul elsewhere refers as babes.[2]

These *babes* are those who have not yet reached full maturity in Christ[3]; so that it is not implausible to suggest further that while the *little ones*, the *weak*, are sometimes those for whom the apostles are responsible, and whom they scandalise at their peril, at other times it is the *weakness* of the apostles themselves which is stressed.[4] In general it is not wrong to say that all Christians are *weak*, for it is only by becoming *a little one* that a man may enter the Kingdom.[5] However that may be, it would be possible to show, were it but relevant here, that St. Paul considered it outrageous presumption for any Christian, himself and the apostles included, to suppose himself anything but a *babe*–for is not the measure of Christian maturity nothing less than Christ himself?[3] But there is no need to prove that he found the *gnostic* struttings of the newly converted Corinthians unedifying to say the least; *puffed-up*[6] is not a pretty word in Greek or English.

The outrage of this presumption reached its height in the matter of idol-meats. The bitter sarcasm of *We know that we all have gnosis*,[7] even without the explicit plea of 10.14 ff is sufficient indication that *weak* throughout this passage appears in inverted commas–'those whom you have the effrontery to despise as weaker brethren'. St. Paul is in general on the side of *the weak*[8] as his Master was; and in this particular matter endorses their attitude. That he alternates a conspiratorial air of superior complicity–'we who know better have to humour the poor things'– with sarcastic rebuke is but pastoral tact. It should not be allowed to conceal Paul's horror at the irresponsible lack of love implied by the action of the self-styled *spiritual*.

In I Cor. 8.10 he writes out in full *the conscience of him who is weak*. What is at issue is not the over-sensitive conscience–it is

---

[1] L. S. Thornton: Essay 'The Body of Christ' in *The Apostolic Ministry*, ed. K. E. Kirk, p. 58 and *passim*.   [2] I Cor. 3.1 f.   [3] Cf. Eph. 4.13.
[4] Thornton, *op. cit.*, p. 55 ff.   [5] Matt. 18.3-4 and parallels.
[6] φυσιοῖ, I Cor. 8.1.   [7] *Ibid.*
[8] I Cor. 9.22; cf. II Cor. 11.29.

undersensitivity that constitutes a defective conscience–but the conscience of the *little one*. The application of the epithet to *conscience* itself in vv. 7 and 12 is no more than a perfectly legitimate telescoping of the longer phrase: the more legitimate in that *conscience* is for St. Paul not a *faculty* or *capacity*[1] of man so much as the whole man in reaction against acts that transgress the limits of his created nature, just as *the Wrath* is a reaction of the external order of things against the transgressor.[2]

The *little one*, then, should be protected by the body of which he is a member, from the pain called *conscience*. It is an offence against love for any other members, even were they genuinely *the strong*[3]–as it is conceivable they might be, but only relatively–to do the opposite. Love alone conduces to edification. To offend against love is to sin against Christ himself[4] whatever may be the moral content of meat-eating considered in isolation; for to consider acts in isolation from the well-being of brother-Christian and neighbour is to abandon the way of Christ.

If one's brother[5] thinks it wrong for a Christian to eat sacrificial meats, then, should he be induced either by example, or by fear of being mocked as 'ignorant', to eat them, he will not be able to free himself sufficiently, from familiarity *until now* with meats as means of communion with idols, not to suffer the pain of conscience. Such is the meaning of both 8.7 and 12. The words for *defile*[6] and *wound*[7] are not so very different from each other as to be much more than alternatives: St. Paul is repeating himself for emphasis and employs them almost as synonyms.[8] Such a *defilement* is painful, and the association of ideas can perhaps best be conveyed by the rendering of 8.7: *the conscience of the little one is scarred*.

The *thus* at the beginning of v. 12 compels the interpretation of v. 10 on the same lines. If this latter verse stood by itself as the sole appearance of *conscience* in the Greek language, let alone in this context, so that we had no external aid to interpretation,

---

[1] Cf. above, pp. 49 ff.   [2] Cf. above, pp. 67 ff.
[3] οἱ δυνατοί; cf. Rom. 15.1.   [4] I Cor. 8.12.
[5] Or neighbour even, if Osborne is right–on I Cor. 10.28 in *J.T.S.* xxxii.167 ff–in supposing the use of ἱερόθυτον to indicate that St. Paul has in mind a pagan informant.
[6] μολύνω, I Cor. 8.7.   [7] τύπτω, *ibid.*, v. 12.
[8] For μιαίνω as a suitable variant description of the result κατὰ συνείδησιν of wrong acts cf. Dion. Halicarn: *de Thuc. jud.* viii.3 (Ex 75) cited above, p. 50.

F

only then would there be any case for asserting that here 'the reference is surely future'.[1] As it is however, we have examined abundant evidence which unanimously indicates the overwhelming probability that *'conscience* in the N.T. is the individual's conscious record of his *past* acts'.[2] We were not able to discover in Greek usage a single case of the reference of any of the συνείδησις group of words to the future.[3] This alone should be enough: but besides that St. Paul in this passage is unquestionably referring to the conscience as the pain (or its seat) consequent upon the inception of an act believed to be wrong. 'Do you call it *edification* of the *weak brother* to lead him by your example, you who claim to have *knowledge,* to eat sacrificial meats and so to bring on the pain of conscience?'[4] is admittedly a paraphrase; but the construction is elliptical, and this interpretation, besides being in accordance with the known use of the word, and with its use in this context, is further justified by the following verse. The weak brother *perisheth.*[5] Christ died to save him from the disease which is causing him to perish–the *conscience* which he suffers *on having done terrible things*; and now this vaunted knowledge has led him once again *to do a terrible thing* (whether or not he be mistaken in supposing the act to be *terrible*) and Christ's work risks being undone. Were it really his *conscience* that St. Paul envisaged as *built-up* no such disastrous consequences would result from his eating. He would no more be *perishing* than those he imitated. It is he himself that is *emboldened* to risk eating, but *his being used until now to the idol*[6] proves too much for him. He eats the meat as sacrificed to idols and thus once again *perisheth*[5] as a result of conscience: for the trouble with conscience is that it is the one pain that cannot be reasoned away.[7] Plausible argument may lead the *little one* astray but it will not so readily quiet his conscience.

The use of *conscience* in Rom. 13.5 is thus exactly what, in a considered exposition, might be expected to emerge from its use in controversy with the Corinthians who first raised it. There

---

[1] J. P. Thornton-Duesbery: *art.* 'Conscience' in *A Theological Word Book of the Bible, ed.* Richardson.

[2] Lake and Cadbury: *Beginnings of Christianity,* IV, p. 286.

[3] Cf. above, pp. 43 ff.   [4] I Cor. 8.10.

[5] ἀπόλλυται, cf. Eur: *Or.* 395 f (Ex 17 and 56) cited above, p. 47, throughout this page.

[6] I Cor. 8.7.

[7] See Plutarch: *de Tranq. Animi* 476F-477A (Ex 49), cited above, p. 47 f.

are certain modifications, but less need for safeguards against possible abuse. The two Corinthians passages show St. Paul granting the need to avoid acts that might lead to conscience, but also adding two considerations as to the reaction of conscience. First, in I Cor. 10 it is to some extent conditioned by accurate knowledge of the moral quality of the act (*ask no questions*): and secondly in I Cor. 8 it is equally to some extent conditioned by habit and environment.[1] *Weak* in the latter passage cannot be pressed into a third consideration–that the conscience can be over-sensitive–beyond the limits of the first.[2] The second consideration is particularly consonant with Rom. 13.5, in that habit, as is well known to moral theology, narrows the limits of a man's internal nature. Even where there is no moral significance, departure from long established habit can produce a reaction not dissimilar from that of conscience.

[1] συνηθείᾳ, I Cor. 8.7.   [2] Cf. above, pp. 79 ff.

IX

THE PAULINE ENVOI

THE undisputedly Pauline writings contain six further occurrences of *conscience*. Two of these, like all those we have examined already, are MBA. Both of them take the form, *conscience bearing witness with*.[1]

In Rom. 9.1 *conscience* is used absolutely and the context is plainly moral. We have already seen that MA is always MBA[2]; St. Paul here makes no breach of that 'Rule'. When he claims that he has 'great sorrow and unceasing pain in [his] heart', no pain smites him internally to accuse him of falsehood. The absence of pain is therefore corroboration, not in itself sufficient but not entirely negligible,[3] of his sincerity. To add conviction to his assertion of his grief for rejected Israel he names both Christ and the Holy Spirit; the former as him who, knowing the hearts of men, must judge his sincerity: the latter as him who, by his indwelling, quickens the sensitivity to the pain of conscience[4] as an internal aspect of man. St. Paul, in an apparently casual use of a commonplace 'understanded of the people' that he addresses, is careful to enrich it by reference to the Spirit. *Conscience*, never perhaps more than a *pis aller*, is doubly inadequate unless the man's moral awareness be quickened by the Spirit, and alert to its responsibility before 'the judgment seat of Christ'.[5] The use here approximates very closely to MBNeg[6]; *I have no painful consciousness of lying*[7] is plainly the corroboration provided by conscience: yet St. Paul leaves this to be inferred from a technically absolute use, and the classification MBA is thus required.

The same phrase in Rom. 2.15 is used rather differently. In 9.1

---

[1] συμμαρτυρούσης τῆς συνειδήσεως, Rom. 2.15 and 9.1.
[2] See above, pp. 24 f, 26 f, 33 ff, etc.
[3] See below, pp. 88 ff on I Cor. 4.4.
[4] Cf. John 16.8 and 9.
[5] Rom. 14.10; II Cor. 5.10.
[6] See below, pp. 94 ff.   [7] I.e. ἐμαυτῷ ψευδόμενος οὐ σύνοιδα.

a particular matter is in point: here generalisations are being made. This accounts for all the differences in emphasis, and it is as mistaken as the assertion that 'St. Paul here writes exactly like a Stoic',[1] of which it is a corollary, to suppose that *conscience* is here identified with *the law written in their hearts*. It is possible of course to see Stoicism here without making such an identification, and many commentators have done so[2]: but even such safeguards as the caveat 'conscience . . . does not make the Law: it recognises it and judges conduct by it'[3]–quite apart from the wrong assumption of Stoic origin which colours them–place more weight on *conscience* than the Greek word St. Paul used is able to bear. St. Paul is at pains to convince his readers, and possibly himself as well, that the Jews, although alone having the Law, have not a monopoly of Law. The Gentiles are members of the same universe, created and governed by the same God.[4] That the Law was revealed to Israel was–despite its grievous limitations–a priceless privilege, carrying with it proportionate responsibilities.[5] But God has not left the Gentiles with no revelation at all. Even were *the invisible things of him* not to be *perceived through the things that are made* there is still *the Wrath* which is *revealed upon all* (and not only Israel's) *ungodliness and unrighteousness of men*.[6] 'And even more than *the Wrath*', St. Paul goes on to say,[7] 'have I not met, universal among the Gentiles, this plainly valid experience of *conscience*, the internal counterpart and complement of *the Wrath*, which adds its vital testimony to my present contention?' That the Gentiles *are a law unto themselves* is shown by three things, distinct but operating in combination. First; their behaviour, their overt acts, reveals that they have accepted standards of some sort for conduct, not entirely other than those of the Jewish Law: secondly; they suffer this pain, conscience, which warns them that they have done or are doing something morally wrong; and thirdly; their reasons pass judgment on their conduct (or, perhaps, in their rational discussions with one another they agree in calling some things right and other things wrong). That by this threefold means some standards of conduct are maintained in theory and practice among the Gentiles is an indication that

---

[1] Dodd: *The Epistle of Paul to the Romans*, p. 36.
[2] E.g. Dodd, *op. cit*; Sanday and Headlam in *ICC, ad loc.*
[3] Dodd, *loc. cit.*   [4] Cf. Acts 17.24 ff, etc.
[5] Rom. 2.17 ff.   [6] *Ibid.*, 1.18 ff; cf. Acts 14.17, etc.   [7] Rom. 2.14 ff.

there is a 'natural Law' derived from the nature of things which is itself a revelation of God's *everlasting power and Divinity*[1] and thus related, through the one God, with the Jewish Law.

Conscience here is again MA, and thus, unless St. Paul departs entirely from the commonplace use of the word, MBA. Had he wished so to depart he would scarcely have failed, at this first occurrence of the word in an Epistle over which he took such pains to make his doctrine clearly understood, to have entered an explanation of the sense in which he was using it, together with an apology for the departure. But did he intend any other sense than the standard MBA the word would be redundant, either repeating the first, or anticipating the third consideration. Deliberately, however, he introduces it as confirmation of the other two, and as distinct from them. Conduct can be merely a matter of convenience; *reasonings*[2] can be tendencious, evasive or simply academic; but conscience,–here is something over which man has sufficiently little control for it to have no little objective validity: pain is convincing where argument is not. That the everyday language of the Gentiles contains a word for confessing to feelings of pain on commission or initiation of particular acts– feelings which carry with them the conviction that the acts ought not to have been committed–is first-hand evidence that the Gentiles are subject, by nature, to a 'natural law' as the Jews, by vocation, to the Torah.

While the undisputedly Pauline writings thus make a consistent use of *conscience* in the MBA sense, there is however an exception to make trial of this rule. In his final letter to the Corinthians St. Paul, after all the troubles and distresses, is only anxious to conciliate. Having, by his 'severe letter', secured the revulsion of feeling in his favour, he is not so tactless as to try to press his advantage too far. At the outset of the dispute *conscience* had been flung in his teeth as justifying certain acts defiant of authoritative regulation.[3] St. Paul has flung it back harder. But now that peace is once again restored, and the Corinthians amenable to his authority, he is careful not to remind them of their discomfiture. He makes but one M use of conscience in II Corinthians and then he applies it to his own conduct,[4] thereby

---

[1] Rom. 1.20.   [2] *Ibid.* 2.15, R.V. mg, for λογισμοί.
[3] See above, pp. 64 f and Cap. VIII.   [4] II Cor. 1.12.

graciously accepting their term for himself. The use he makes
of it however is quite different. 'Our glorying', he says, 'is this';
and then, when he could have passed immediately to the clause[1]
that gives the content of his *glorying*, he pauses to make, deliberately, room for the insertion in parenthesis of the conciliatory use
of *conscience*: 'that is, the testimony of our conscience, that in
holiness and sincerity of God, not in fleshly wisdom but in the
grace of God we behaved ourselves.' This is straightforward
MPG–a rare use of συνείδησις, if it occurs at all outside the N.T.,
although found a little more frequently of αὐτῷ συνειδέναι and of
τὸ συνειδός. Its rarity, as we remarked, is surprising in view of
its naturalness as an extension of MBNorm.[2] Still more rare is
the construction used to define the content of conscience.[1] These
two rarities are more than rarities in the N.T. period–no parallel
can be found outside the N.T. even approximately contemporary.
St. Paul seems to have taken the trouble to go to the utmost possible M limits of *conscience* to avoid hurting the Corinthians' feelings.

To suggest that *holiness*, *sincerity* and *grace*–all richly positive
words–are secondary and stand here in answer merely to the
charge of behaviour *in fleshly wisdom*, the main concern of the
clause being to deny that St. Paul has such behaviour 'on his
conscience', is scarcely to do justice to his ingenuity and tact.
Nevertheless it is worth remarking on this single MBNeg appear-
ing in the midst of the threefold MPG, if only because it shows
clearly how the route runs from MBA and Norm to MPG
through MBNeg.

The other two appearances of συνείδησις in II Corinthians[3]
should not be rendered *conscience* at all. Perhaps St. Paul again is
deliberately demonstrating that the word can be used inoffen-
sively: be that as it may, both are certainly NA here. Whereas
συνείδησις is only *conscience* in so far as it represents αὐτῷ συνειδέναι,
in neither of these cases is there any possibility whatever of a
reflexive. In both of them what is in question is the knowledge
that *others* have of *our* conduct; in the one case: 'all men know
that we have not handled the word of God deceitfully'; in the
other: 'you know as well as we do that we preach in fear of God

---

[1] Introduced by ὅτι. For the extreme rarity of this means of defining the content
of συνείδησις cf. above, p. 21, n. 3, on Plato: *Symp.* 216ᵃ (Ex 4).
[2] See the statistics set out on p. 35 above, n. 1.   [3] II Cor. 4.2 and 5.11.

and do not tamper with the gospel for the sake of human popularity.' It is thus clear that here it is the simple σύνοιδα that is represented, and not αὐτῷ συνειδέναι.[1]

The first word that St. Paul wrote on *conscience* should now be allowed to have the last word, before we pass to the examination of less certainly Pauline writings. In I Cor. 4.4[2] there is a caveat entered that is not only an essential corrective to any impression that might be gained of St. Paul's idea of the *conscience* from his other uses, particularly those immediately above, in II Corinthians, but also of great significance in assessing the place of *conscience* in a Christian ethic. St. Paul writes, in the context of a rejection of human judgment: 'I have nothing on my conscience, yet am I not hereby justified.'[3] This is the familiar MBNeg use of the basic verbal phrase: even if St. Paul did not hear it often—for by this time the noun was the more common usage—and even if, *per impossibile*, he had not read the LXX version of Job 27.6[4] —he nevertheless not only manages the phrase with a practised hand, but also penetrates immediately to the great defect in conscience as a moral safeguard. The English AV with its correct but archaic translation 'I know nothing by myself'–*by* here being an earlier equivalent of the R.V.'s *against*–doubly obscures the connection with *conscience* for the modern reader. I have rendered the passage by 'I have nothing on my conscience . . .'. It could equally well be rendered 'my conscience is clear . . .' or even 'I have a good conscience . . .'[5]–in order to convey, what was obvious to the Corinthian reader, the close relation of συνείδησις with ἐμαυτῷ σύνοιδα. *Conscience* has been introduced into the argument by the Corinthians: at the outset of his reply, then, St. Paul issues this solemn warning. 'Only the Lord, at the consummation, can adequately assess the quality of acts and of the character they both express and produce. It is rash and wrong, therefore, for him to presume to judge others, who cannot judge even himself.' There are, of course, sources of error in conscience itself. These St. Paul introduces in their place–inaccurate knowledge of the quality of the act,[6] habit, environment,[7] imperfect awareness of Christ as judge, and of the standard which he

---

[1] Cf. Dem: *de Corona* 110 (Ex 36), cited p. 30, above.   [2] Cf. above, pp. 64 f.
[3] οὐδὲν γὰρ ἐμαυτῷ σύνοιδα, ἀλλ' οὐκ ἐν τούτῳ δεδικαίωμαι.   [4] Cf. above, p. 55.
[5] Cf. above, pp. 25 ff, 36 ff.   [6] See above, p. 77.   [7] See above, p. 83.

embodies and by which he must judge; and insufficient quickening of the inner man by the indwelling of the Holy Spirit[1]–but he is not referring to them here. The defect of conscience as an ethical norm is common to every man: even if in all other respects it is 'functioning perfectly' it still remains negative only. Conscience comes into operation when the moral limits of a man's own nature are transgressed[2]: but the simplest way to avoid walking over an edge is to stand still. The demands of God are positive, according to St. Paul–standing still is rebuked as sternly by Jesus in the parable of the talents as gross sin.[3] Even if–perhaps *per impossibile*–the 'silence' of conscience can be taken to mean that a man has done nothing wrong, it can never be assumed from it that he has been accounted righteous. This rendering is preferred to such negative versions as 'My conscience is not uneasy–not that that acquits me'[4] or 'an unaccusing conscience does not *per se* mean absence of guilt'[5] because, despite the use of the forensic metaphor, St. Paul by *justification* always implied the award of a status of real and positive righteousness–the righteousness, in fact, of Christ–by virtue of incorporation into him. If the terms of our analysis be employed, St. Paul is saying, 'The assumption that MBNeg is necessarily MPG is unwarrantable.' In terms of homiletic it can most clearly be paraphrased: 'The onset of the pain of conscience must always, certainly, be taken as proof that the sufferer has done something wrong. The absence of such pain does not mean that he has done something right or good. It may mean that he has done nothing at all; or it may mean that he has in some way deadened his capacity[6] to feel this pain to a greater or lesser extent–that in fact, his conscience is defective.' It should of course be borne in mind that neither Greek popular thought, nor the N.T. writers, were much preoccupied with such analysis as we have attempted. The basic conception of *conscience* as *pain*,[7] *disease*[8] or *ulcer*,[7] allowed the word to be used indifferently not only as the pain itself–but also as the capacity to feel such pain, and as the 'agent' or instrument whereby the pain is in-

[1] See above, p. 84 f.   [2] Cf. above, p. 68 ff, on Rom. 13.5.
[3] Matt. 25.14-30 (Luke 19.11-27). Cf. Matt. 8.12, 22.13.
[4] W. F. Howard in *Abingdon Commentary*, ad loc.
[5] Robertson and Plummer in *ICC, ad loc.*
[6] Cf. below, p. 91 ff on I Tim. 4.2.
[7] Cf. Plutarch: *de Tranq. Animi* 476F-477A (Ex 49) cited above, p. 47
[8] Cf. Eur: *Or.* 395 f (Ex 17 and 56), cited above, p. 47.

flicted.[1] If St. Paul uses the word dominantly as connoting the simple pain,[2] he also can think of it as an *agent*.[3] The *capacity* aspect is perhaps latent in I Cor. 8.7 ff but for the most part is confined to the more doubtfully Pauline uses, particularly in the Pastoral epistles.[4] But we should not forget that the word always represents a compound verb, of which he who commits the act is the subject, and in which the συν- governs the reflexive pronoun. That St. Paul here uses the verbal phrase in the normal Greek way shows that he was well aware of this.

[1] See above, pp. 48 ff.
[2] I.e. the διὰ τὴν συνείδησιν passages, Rom. 13.5; I Cor. 10.25, 27-29; also I Cor. 8.7, 10, 12.
[3] I.e. the use συμμαρτυρούσης τῆς συνειδήσεως, Rom. 2.15, 9.1; cf. II Cor. 1.12.
[4] Cf. below, Chapter Ten.

X

CONSCIENCE AND FAITH

Perhaps the outstanding example of the *capacity* or *faculty*[1] image of *conscience* is I Tim. 4.2. The word rendered by the R.V. *branded . . . with a hot iron*[2] is very rare. It and the other words of the same family[3] are, it is true, all found in connection with *branding*: but they are also found in medical and veterinary writers in connection presumably with therapeutic cauterisation.[4] Decisive proof may be lacking for either interpretation here, so that A.V. is wiser than its successor in confining itself to the literal and non-committal rendering *seared*. . . . Therapeutic cauterisation was, however, scarcely less familiar to the first-century A.D. than branding, and the use of *their own*[5] suggests that the voice of the perfect participle here is not passive but middle, and *their own conscience* thus, more naturally, its object, and not an accusative of respect. While branding is essentially that to which a man is subjected by another, he might well cauterise himself.

The use here, however, is in any case metaphorical, so that precise definition of the type of cauterisation envisaged is perhaps lost labour; it is the effect of such treatment that matters, and that is always the same—loss of sensitivity in the area treated. The natural interpretation of such metaphorical use is *made callous*[6]; and support is given to such an interpretation by the laboriousness and the amount of importation of ideas in no way

---

[1] See above, pp. 49 f. [2] κεκαυτηριασμένων.

[3] e.g.: καυτήρ: καυτήριον: καυστικός, κτλ.

[4] Galen (*Ed* Kühn xix.111) refers to καυτήρ and καυτηρίδιον in his glossary of medical terms and surgical instruments. Although the definitions do not specify the use to which they should be put, this can hardly be supposed to be concerned with *branding*. Detailed instruction in how and when to cauterise in the treatment of equine ailments is given in *Hippiatri Berolini* 288 to 295; the sole certain use of the passive of καυτηριάζω occurs in *Hippiatri* 1. It is also of interest that *Hipp. Berol.* xcvi.13 is a prescription for a *caustic* preparation to be used to desensitise (equine) ulcers (i.e. ἑλκῶν–cf. Plutarch: *de Tranq. Anim.* 476F-477A (Ex 49), cited above, p. 47 f).

[5] I.e. τὴν ἰδίαν συνείδησιν. [6] *Concise Oxford English Dictionary sub* 'cauterise'.

warranted by the Greek, involved in the *branding* interpretation. The least laboured is *bearing the indelible mark of unrepented sin.*[1] Beyond, however, the strict limits of translation, or even of paraphrase, are such renderings as *branded with the brand of slavery to their master Satan*[2]; *like branded slaves knowing their guilt*[3] or *branded by Satan and aware of it in their conscience.*[4] Such interpretations in any case do not take into account the idea of conscience as normally a pain or disease,[5] which creates a strong presumption in favour of the surgical image.

The course of action in point[6] is a deliberate rejection first of *the faith*, then of God, and next of truth and honesty: the apostates are going to place themselves at the disposal of the angels of *The Deceiver*.[7] But they are going to be apostates,[8] that is, they have known the Truth, and have been influenced by the best environment,[9] for they will be 'ex-Christians'.[10] Thus this course of action must be expected to result in agonising reactions of conscience unless prior action has been taken to anaesthetise the capacity for so suffering–hence the use of the perfect participle. The author takes it for granted that such a career could not be embarked upon unless those who did so were already completely under the anaesthetic, or, rather, had *with a hot iron* completely destroyed the 'nerve-endings'.

Tit. 1.15 envisages a similar situation. The author, in referring to conscience as *defiled*, departs slightly from Pauline usage. We saw that St. Paul used a word virtually equivalent, to express the effect of (what was supposed to be) sin on the conscience.[11] Here again the effect of sin on the conscience is in point, but the sin concerned is no longer a single act, it is a *habitus*. The characters concerned are completely corrupted: the desire for virtue, of which for the Christian the emulation of Christ's example is the

---

[1] Brown in *Westminster Commentary*, *ad loc*: he refers to the *FVR* brand of the convicted thief.

[2] Lock in *ICC*, *ad loc*.   [3] Humphreys in *Cambridge Bible*, *ad loc*.

[4] Scott in *Moffatt Commentary*, *ad loc*–but he plainly prefers the *cautery* interpretation.

[5] Cf. above, pp. 45 ff.   [6] I Tim. 4.1 f.   [7] Cf. Rev. 12.9.

[8] Cf. ἀποστήσονται: I Tim. 4.1.   [9] Cf. p. 83, above.

[10] *pace*, of course, those who insist that 'ex-Christian' is a contradiction; that apostasy is proof that those guilty of it were never really Christians at all.

[11] I Cor. 8.7 ff in which μολύνω is in the context virtually a synonym for τύπτω; and the use of both is parallel to that of μιαίνω in Dion. Halicarn: *de Thuc. jud.* viii.3 (Ex 75), cited above, p. 50, n. 3.

higher equivalent, and which is the prerequisite of the hatred of sin, has completely[1] disappeared. They claim to know God (thus *unbelieving*[2] here must mean *apostates*) but by their works they deny him (or, more probably, their claim). The two last safeguards of their human nature as such are, therefore, it is plain, also completely corrupted. This is the necessary preliminary[3]: so long as some vestiges of *mind* and *conscience* remain no man can be called (completely) *defiled*. *Seared with a hot iron* would be the preferable, because the less confusing, image; the use of *defile* here, however, does serve to show clearly how the author—who at the least wishes to represent St. Paul's teaching—conceives the work of *cauterisation* to be accomplished.[4] A single (supposedly) wrong act, according to his master, *wounds* or *defiles* the conscience—smites it and leaves a scar.[5] If this sin be not repented and repudiated, and if other sins be committed, the *conscience* becomes in time all *scar* and no *conscience*. It is when it is thus completely *defiled* that it ceases to be effective in its proper office: it is callous or cauterised. If the *Romans* image be employed,[6] each assault on the created limits of man's nature weakens them; if they be not repaired after each assault at the last they become so elastic, or are beaten down so low, that they can be overstepped with impunity. In medical parlance, by repeated intake of a poison the system's tolerance of it is increased.[7] It is not irrelevant to observe that while tolerance is increased, the need for larger and larger quantities and more and more frequent intake is increased also. Beyond a certain stage the addict is subject-matter for the pathologist, for the *form*, as an older wisdom would have said, that constituted him as distinguishably man has been disintegrated. He has become once more *without form and void*.[8] In so far as he still embodies anything, he embodies no more than a craving for the particular poison. Thus Tit. 1.15 points rightly to the corollary both of that passage itself and of I Tim. 4.2: not only the *conscience* but also that of which it is but the negative and complementary counterpart, the *mind* is made null. It is important to observe the emphatic and deliberate distinction made between these two aspects of the moral nature of man by the use in Greek

---

[1] The perfect tense is again used: μεμιασμένοις; μεμίανται.　　[2] I.e. ἄπιστοι.
[3] Cf. above, p. 92, on I Tim. 4.2.　　[4] Cf. Lock in *ICC*, *ad loc.*
[5] Cf. above, pp. 81 f, on I Cor. 8.7 ff.　　[6] Cf. above, pp. 67 ff on Rom. 13.5.
[7] Cf. Housman: *A Shropshire Lad*, LXII.　　[8] Cf. Gen. 1.2 and pp. 68 ff, above.

of the double *and*.[1] They are the two bulwarks without which that nature collapses into decomposition[2]; the one is positive but subjective, recognises order, and decides duties in accordance with it; the other is negative but objective, and reacts painfully to infringements of order. Of the two *conscience* is the latter resort. *Mind* can be so often beclouded otherwise than by sin–by inadequate knowledge of the facts, by honest error, by defective logic. It is, in fallen man, the earlier to be breached. *Conscience* is the last line of defence, itself a negative thing, a *pis aller*, but better than nothing. So the passage stresses the completeness of the corruption of the *unbelieving*: not only the *mind* is reduced to ineffectuality–but also the *conscience*. That this is a deliberate crescendo is obvious, not only from the double *and*, but more particularly by the inversion of the order to bring *conscience* to the end of the sentence.[1] A man may be able neither to recognise what is right, nor to see what he should do next, without being lost beyond recall. When his conscience–here his capacity to suffer when he transgresses his Divinely-fixed limits–is gone, then all is gone. Only the perfect tense can express his condition: he is the opposite of saved[3]–he is *unto every good work reprobate*.[4]

Six 'Pauline A' occurrences of *conscience* have been classified MBNeg. In all of them the writer assumes that his readers are familiar with the word and the idea that it connotes, and thus will require no explanation. In each case an epithet is attached, in three cases ἀγαθή, in two καθαρά and in one ἀπρόσκοπος.[5] The last two both imply negation of what would normally arouse conscience, καθαρή implying the removal of stain, and ἀπρόσκοπος either the absence of any *stumbling* on the part of the subject himself, or that he has not set any *occasion of stumbling* in another's way.[6] This, taken in conjunction with the evidence of the Greek sources which we have already exhaustively discussed[7] creates a strong presumption in favour of the MBNeg interpretation of the three ἀγαθή occurrences.

In Acts 24.16 St. Paul is represented as making his defence against charges brought by *Ananias and certain elders* who are present, but before a Gentile governor,[8] who is, however,

---

[1] μεμίανται αὐτῶν καὶ ὁ νοῦς καὶ ἡ συνείδησις.
[2] Cf. p. 92 ff, immediately above.　　　[3] i.e. σεσωσμένος.　　　[4] Tit. 1.16.
[5] See the analysis on p. 62　　　[6] Cf. immediately below, p. 95, n. 3.
[7] See above, pp. 25 ff, 35 ff, etc.　　　[8] Acts 24.1.

relatively familiar with Judaism.[1] The charge is summed up under the comprehensive symbol of 'profanation of the Temple'.[2] The charge, found to be effective with Pilate, of insurrection, is scouted by St. Paul: he knows that there is no proof and that Felix will ignore it. In answer to the real case against him he protests that he has neither broken the Law nor by word nor example persuaded other Jews to break it. His concern, the author makes him say, and if St. Luke had not read Romans and Corinthians he at least appears to have been familiar with St. Paul's mind in the matter, has been always to avoid having *offences on his conscience*. The meaning of the passage is not affected by whether *void of offence* here be transitive or intransitive; the English versions wisely evade the issue, and the meaning of *conscience* here, and its classification as MBNeg, remain the same whichever view be preferred.[3]

Addressing Jews only in Acts 23.1 St. Paul is not represented as using the word ἀπρόσκοπος but ἀγαθή. The meaning, however, is not dissimilar. He is under the same arrest as in the later passage, and on the same charge[4]: it is only the audience that is different, in that no Gentile magistrate presides. Consequently he insists that as a member of God's people he has not, so far as conscience can tell, transgressed its laws and usages. In an analogy with I Cor. 8, wherein it was seen that *the weak conscience* meant *the conscience of the little one* by a transference of the epithet, it is possible that the quality of the man is here transferred to the conscience.[5] Thus this passage could be paraphrased: 'Conscience does not pain me for any falling-short of the duty of a good citizen of God's people.'[6] The negative character of this defence is sufficient to justify the classification MBNeg. It is forced on St. Paul by the circumstances; he can hardly claim to be a 'good

---

[1] Acts 24.10 f.   [2] *Ibid.*, v.6.

[3] Cf. Lake and Cadbury: *Beginnings of Christianity, ad loc.* Some grounds for taking it transitively appear from a comparison of Rom. 14.13 ff with I Cor. 10.31 ff. ἀπρόσκοποι in the latter passage, interpreted by the former, must mean μὴ τιθέντες πρόσκομμα. The combination of to *Jews and Greeks* in I Cor. 10.32 makes the interpretation of ἀπρόσκοπον συνείδησιν ἔχειν in the present passage as μηδὲν ἐμαυτῷ συνειδέναι πρόσκομμα θείς particularly attractive in view of the circumstances under which St. Paul had to plead.   [4] Cf. Acts 21.28.

[5] Here and in the other two ἀγαθή occurrences the suggestion of Osborne (*J.T.S.* xxxii.167 ff) is helpful, in addition to the evidence available.

[6] Cf. Phil. 3.6, in which it is significant that St. Paul's claim in respect of *the righteousness which is in the law* is thus negative–i.e. ἄμεμπτος.

Jew' any longer[1] but he will assert that he hasn't been a bad one, a law-breaker.

Void of offence applied to *conscience* if transitive means 'free from the sin against others of leading them astray'; if intransitive it means simply 'free from sin' in a sense to be understood by both Jew and Gentile. *Good* in Acts 23.1 means 'free from the guilt of profanation of the Jewish Religion'. In the Pastorals, whether good[2] or pure[3] be used, the meaning is simply 'free from (conscious) sin'.[4] This is obviously the case where *pure* is used. In I Tim. 3.9 *a pure conscience* is used to sum up the avoidance of three wrong practices that is incumbent on *the Deacon*; while in II Tim. 1.3 the author represents by it the Pauline *blameless*.[5] It is hardly less obvious where *good* is used. In both cases the object of St. Paul's *charge*[6] to Timothy is being stated. In I Tim. 1.5 *love* is the *end* of all pastoral ministry, represented in this case by *the charge*. Such love must proceed from an *unfeigned faith*, and, on the moral side, from a *pure* intention and its negative aspect, the avoidance of conscious sin.[7] In I Tim. 1.19 neither *love*, nor *heart* is mentioned, but *a good conscience* is still the pair to *faith*. It must still mean *avoidance of sin*, for it is evident that this second passage is but a shorter recapitulation of the first; not only from *charge* nor even from *faith . . . good conscience*, but also from the results which the author forsees of the abandonment of the pattern of life enjoined in the charge. In both cases it is *shipwreck concerning the faith*, but 1.6 goes into the literal detail of what is meant by this metaphor in 1.19. *Swerved from*[8] and *thrust away*[9] are thus two further figures, under which the treatment of *conscience* by apo-

---

[1] Cf. Acts 21.20 ff.　　[2] I.e. ἀγαθή, I Tim. 1.5 and 19.

[3] I.e. καθαρά, I Tim. 3.9; II Tim. 1.3.

[4] Justice is of course not done to *conscience*, unless the element of *consciousness*, which the Greek form of the word never allowed its users to forget be duly recognised. Cf. Philo: *QDSI* 128 (Ex 47), cited above, p. 49.

[5] I.e. ἄμεμπτος, cf. Phil. 3.6 and p. 95, n. 6, above.

[6] παραγγελία, I Tim. 1.5 and 18; although in the former case it is for Timothy to pass it on (cf. παραγγείλῃς *ibid.*, v. 3) it is still Paul's charge to him in the first place.

[7] This may be an over-pressing of what is perhaps no more than an otiose repetition for homiletic purposes. I doubt this, as *unfeigned faith* is patently not such a repetition: but if it is so then καρδία is virtually the equivalent of συνείδησις, and thus καθαρά of ἀγαθή.　　[8] I.e. ἀστοχήσαντες, I Tim. 1.5.

[9] I.e. ἀπωσάμενοι, *ibid.*, v. 19. This is so even if ἥν be taken to refer to ἀγαθήν συνείδησιν; to πίστιν . . . συνείδησιν, or even to στρατείαν rather than to συνείδησιν alone. In any case the middle voice should be noticed; cf. above, p. 91 f, on κεκαυτηριασμένων.

states, actual or potential, is described, to add to *defiled*[1] and *seared with a hot iron*.[2] All four significantly assume the interplay of *conscience* with *faith*. Faith informs conscience,[3] but outrages to conscience are a preliminary to an abandonment of the faith.[4]

The Pastorals consistently employ the 'capacity-image' of *conscience*[5]: but this image always implies in Greek, and the Pastorals are no exception, the capacity to feel pain on committing a wrong act. A man is in better health, when his disease decreases in severity, and in good health when he has no disease: a *good conscience* is the absence of this pain from the man who has the capacity to feel it. *Acts* is similar to the Pastorals in this respect, and both are therefore here at least not word-perfect in their representation of St. Paul; they nevertheless fall well within the limits of the Greek commonplace usage from which he was compelled by the Corinthians to adopt the word.

The N.T. contains but two further instances of the use of the phrase *a good conscience*.[6] Although these do not occur in even possibly Pauline writings but in I Peter,[7] discussion of them belongs in this chapter, and in any case is easier with the usage of the Pastoral Epistles fresh in our minds.

I have set I Peter 3.16 on the borderline between MBNeg and MPG because here the phrase occurs in the context of an exhortation to irreproachable conduct as the most effective witness to the faith.[8] Nevertheless the phrase itself is negative, meaning, as it does in the Pastoral Epistles, *the avoidance of conscious sin*[9]; and, while my *irreproachable* is perhaps a tendencious periphrasis for *good* in the final clause, yet plainly what the author desires is that the non-believer should not be able to find any fault in the Christian, and that, to this end, the Christian should not be (painfully) aware of any faults in himself.

The phrase occurs again five verses later in one of the most notable of the N.T.'s *cruces interpretum*.[10] The context, while

---

[1] I.e. μεμίανται, Tit. 1.15; see p. 92 ff, above.
[2] I.e. κεκαυτηριασμένων, I Tim. 4.2; see p. 91 f, above.
[3] Cf. Rom. 9.1, in which this office is performed by Christ and the Holy Spirit.
[4] Cf. ματαιολογίαν, I Tim. 1.6; περὶ τὴν πίστιν ἐναυάγησαν, *ibid.*, v. 19; ἀποστήσονται τῆς πίστεως, *ibid.*, 4.1; and ἄπιστοι, Tit. 1.15. The *defilement* of νοῦς, in the last passage is aptly elaborated by the first—μὴ νοοῦντες . . . κτλ., I Tim. 1.7.
[5] See pp. 49 f, above.   [6] I.e. ἀγαθὴ συνείδησις.   [7] I Peter 3.16 and 21.
[8] ζηλωταὶ τοῦ ἀγαθοῦ, *ibid.*, v. 13, cannot fail to recall Xen: *Cyr.* I.v.11 (Ex 8), cited above, p. 23. Cf. also ἀγαθὴν ἀναστροφήν (*ibid.*, v. 16) and ἀγαθοποιοῦντας (*ibid.*, v. 17).   [9] See above, pp. 96.   [10] I Peter 3.21.

G

following easily from what went before, is now the once-for-all efficacy of Christ's suffering for sin, and the relation to it of Christian initiation. The *flood* and *ark* figure is something of a misfit of baptism: for the flood-waters were, not the means of deliverance but, the quintessence of *the Wrath*, of God's judgment in external action, by natural calamity, against the sins of men.[1] From this external *wrath* those within the ark were delivered, so that this strange vessel is a type of the Church, sealed in stone, to this day. But we have already seen that *the Wrath* has an internal complement and counterpart–*conscience*.[2] However ἐπερώτημα is to be interpreted, therefore, let alone translated, the meaning of *conscience* is still that with which we are by now familiar. As entry into the Ark separated the eight souls, so initiation into the Church separates the Christian, from the sinful world and the wrath impending over it. This initiation, however, unlike that earlier entry, includes also an internal deliverance among its effects. The MBA conscience, the internal and personal aspect of *the Wrath*, is by baptism–that is, by the appropriation of the saving efficacy of Christ's passion to the individual, and not by his own renunciation of the filth of the flesh–negatived to MBNeg.

This interpretation of the relation of conscience to the mystery of redemption is here suggested rather than stated–and that obscurely and in passing. It is fully expounded and developed, as one of its key themes, by the *Epistle to the Hebrews*, which sees *conscience* against the background of the same themes–the once-for-all efficacy of Christ's death, and Christian initiation. To that Epistle, as setting the crown on the N.T. use of *conscience*, we must now turn.

---

[1] Cf. above, pp. 67 ff.   [2] Cf. above, pp. 70 ff.

XI

CONSCIENCE AND ATONEMENT

ST. PAUL took the Greek idea of *conscience* into Christianity because he had no choice; it was an element of the urgent problem at Corinth. His first reaction had been immediately to perceive both the liability of conscience to error through defective knowledge of the moral quality of acts, or through environment and habit, and its major defect as an ethical norm, its negativity. The disturbances at Corinth had been sufficient to indicate these, and to make him, while granting the point to the Corinthians, a little harsh in his treatment of the subject; so that he tried in his last surviving letter to them to introduce a conciliatory softening of it. Dissatisfied with this attempt, he reduced his ideas on *conscience* to order in Romans–an epistle of which the watchword might well have been 'No loose ends'–but gave it no very prominent position. Altogether in these three epistles he leaves *conscience* very much as he found it, making only that minimum of adjustment necessary to make it fit within the framework of those doctrines of God, creation and man which he presupposed in his preaching of the Gospel.

The Pastoral Epistles and Acts introduced it as a Pauline word, but differed from their model in preferring MBNeg to MBA. They develop the idea by pointing to an interplay of faith with conscience such that a virtual destruction of the capacity for the latter is the necessary preliminary to an abandonment of the former. Two of the occurrences of συνείδησις in I Peter exemplify the same usage as that in the Pastoral Epistles and St. Paul's speeches in Acts; we will discuss the third Petrine occurrence later.[1]

While all these occurrences of *conscience* are consistent with its use in contemporary and popular Greek, its treatment is through-

---

[1] see below, pp. 105 ff.

out little more than peripheral to the main stream of doctrine. The author *to the Hebrews*, however, integrates it most skilfully with the exposition of his theme.

It is no part of our present concern to discuss either the identity of the author or the background of those to whom this marvellous sermon is addressed. It must suffice to say that, whoever he was, the writer understood *conscience* and appreciated it far more than either St. Paul or his imitators. His use of it is sparing, but the more effective by virtue of that telling economy. Using the word only five times he nevertheless contrives so to develop his theme that he can move in orderly progression through all the categories of its use that were current coin in the Greek world.[1] Justice is not done to this skilful development by attempts to interpret his use solely by the other N.T. occurrences[2]; for the N.T., apart from this epistle, does not use MBNorm, nor does its usage, taken in isolation, sufficiently show that it is the norm assumed in MBA and MBNeg. Still less, of course, can it indicate the vital distinction within συνείδησις, between αὐτῷ συνειδέναι and the simple συνειδέναι.[3]

The starting point for *Hebrews* is the axiom 'that man cannot worship God with a (guilty) conscience'.[4] The author has set himself to show, on the presuppositions of the Levitical religion itself, that Christianity, accomplishing fully what the former accomplishes only partially if at all, is the better religion.[5] Interspersing his argument with much digressive homiletic, he compares Christ with the prophets[6]; with the angels[7], and with

[1] I.e. MBA (9.9); MBNorm (9.14 and 10.22); MBNeg (10.2); and MBNeg/MPG (13.18). The insertion of the second MBNorm (10.22) after the first MBNeg (10.2), at first sight a break in the progression, will be seen on examination to be a *tour de force*, a sort of theological syncopation: see p. 102 below.

[2] Cf. Westcott on 9.9.   [3] See above, pp. 18 ff, 29 f, 87 f and below, p. 105 ff.

[4] So Narborough, *The Clarendon Bible*, on Heb. 9.9. I have placed *guilty* in brackets as it is not represented in the Greek; cf. also Moffatt in *ICC*, *ad loc.*, who renders συνείδησιν by *consciousness of sin*. *Of sin* or *guilty* have to be supplied in English to make the point clear. συνείδησις is here MBA (for κατὰ συνείδησιν; cf. above, p. 50, n. 1) which assumes *sin* as the normal content, and must be interpreted as 'the painful consciousness that a man has of his own past sin'; not the least part of the pain is the inability to worship God which it entails.

[5] There are some grounds for supposing that the author is taking the Levitical system as the inclusive type of all religions other than Christianity. In any case he regards Christianity as the best of all, indeed as the only effective religion, precisely in that it alone deals effectively with what he regards as the crucial problem—the (MBA) conscience, which all others fail to solve, even if they recognise it as such, as the Levitical certainly did, though not in these terms.

[6] Heb. 1.1-3.   [7] *Ibid.*, 1.4-14.

Moses.[1] After these necessary preliminaries he reaches, with the introduction of the Melchizedek motif[2], the core of his argument.

He expounds the High Priesthood of Melchizedek, as prefiguring Christ's, and then contrasts Christ's priesthood with the Aaronic. When, next, the New Ritual is being contrasted with the Old, the time has at length come to inject *conscience* into the framework. As the Old Ritual 'cannot, as touching the conscience, make the worshipper perfect',[3] 'the way into the holy place hath not yet been made manifest'[4], and there is no open access to God in worship. The coming of Christ, however, puts an end to this dilemma[5]. In him there is at last the assurance that conscience shall be cleansed from *dead works*[6]: in principle it is now possible for man 'to serve the living God'[7] entering, with serene confidence, into *the holy place*.[8] Until this deliverance is appropriated by men they have no choice but to continue offering 'the same sacrifices year by year',[9] although this repetition is itself proof that they offer in vain. Did the worshipper once achieve by his sacrifices that which he sought by their means, the condition of having 'no more conscience of sins',[10] he would offer them no longer. Thus only 'where there is remission (of *sins and iniquities*)' is there 'no more offering for sin'.[11] This remission is only won 'by the blood of Jesus'[12]: the *once-for-all*[13] efficacy of the one perfect sacrifice having done away the only obstacle, the *evil conscience*, the individual, appropriating it by his incorporation into Christ,[14] can at last 'draw near' to God in worship 'with a true heart in fulness of faith'.[15]

The way in which the author employs all five possible M uses of συνείδησις to point the absolute efficacy of Christ's death may thus be set out in a scheme of five stages.

Stage 1: (MBA–Heb. 9.9). Conscience is the real obstacle to worship. The ritual of the Old Covenant, although well aware of this, is powerless to deliver from conscience, so that would-be worshippers are frustrated of their object and have no open access to God.

---

[1] Heb. 3.1-6.　　　[2] *Ibid.*, 6.20.
[3] μὴ δυνάμεναι κατὰ συνείδησιν τελειῶσαι τὸν λατρεύοντα, *ibid.*, 9.9.
[4] *Ibid.*, 9.8.　　[5] *Ibid.*, 9.11.　　[6] *Ibid.*, 9.14; N.B. the future tense of καθαριεῖ.
[7] *Ibid.*　[8] *Ibid.*, 10.19.　[9] *Ibid.*, 10.1.　[10] *Ibid.*, 10.2.　[11] *Ibid.*, 10.18.　[12] *Ibid.*, 10.19.
[13] ἐφάπαξ *ibid.*, 10.10, and *passim.*
[14] The reference to Christian initiation, *ibid.*, 10.22, is unmistakable.
[15] *Ibid.*, 10.22.

Stage 2: (MBNorm–Heb. 9.14). Christ's sacrifice, in contrast, has done away conscience *of dead works*, so that in him is offered the assurance that those shall be delivered from their frustration, who are incorporated in Him.

Stage 3: (MBNeg–Heb. 10.2). Against the background of this assured future deliverance from, or negation of, conscience, the futility of the repetition characteristic of the Old Ritual is emphasised. So long as the worshipper seeks negation by these useless means he is doomed to remain under the pain of the MBNorm conscience.

Stage 4: (MBNorm–Heb. 10.22). Once, however, by submitting to Christian initiation, he has fully appropriated the benefits of Christ's passion,[1] he can look back with thanksgiving on his former MBNorm conscience from which he is now happily at last delivered. He can embark on that *new and living way*[2] by which he has open access to God in worship.[3]

The actual condition of his conscience is in *Stages* 1 *to* 3 MBA and MBNorm: only in *Stage* 4 does it become, in Christ, MBNeg. The brilliant inversion of the usage in *Stages* 3 *and* 4 serves to bring out the contrast between the dreary futility of the former's quest for the negation of conscience by any means other than Christ; and the latter's triumphant joy of deliverance *once for all*. *Stage* 3 looks forward to *Stage* 4 but ever in vain apart from Christ's sacrifice: *Stage* 4 looks back on *Stage* 3 as on a nightmare from which a man has awoken to find himself in his own true home.

Stage 5: (MBNeg/MPG–Heb. 13.18). The crown is now put on the series. With great skill the writer presses on to the upper limit of the possible use of *conscience*. In Christ the pain is, from the first, done away: and, in him, the Christian, as he grows, may hope that its place may be taken more and more by joy. The writer, however, is not prepared to press, even now, beyond the borderline: he is content to show that the Christian life moves steadily away from the pain of conscience. Thus while he uses the epithet *good*[4] he qualifies the whole sentence with *we are persuaded*–words expressing something less than final certainty, but

---

[1] The perfect tenses of ἐρραντισμένοι and λελουμένοι should be noticed.
[2] Heb. 10.20.
[3] With Heb. 10.22 cf. Ep. Barn. 19.12: οὐ προσήξεις ἐπὶ προσευχὴν ἐν συνειδήσει πονηρᾷ and see above p. 100, n. 4.   [4] καλήν, cf. καλῶς ἀναστρέφεσθαι.

rather, in hope and faith, a sober confidence: and *good* itself he qualifies with a parenthesis which, by the use of *desiring*, indicates that the *to live honestly in all things* is of intention and aspiration rather than of accomplishment. Further, the whole sentence is introduced by *for*, following a request for prayer on his behalf. In fact he knows conscience too well, and has already used it too decisively as MBA, to claim unequivocally that it can ever be a positive and pleasurable index of virtue: but at least it no longer besets him, and he has the joy of open access to God in worship at last.

That this claim is put in the first person is not surprising. The writer is exercising his office as shepherd, albeit derivatively.[1] He calls the sheep not to stray but to follow him. If they wander back over the way they have so far travelled they will, at length, again suffer the torments of conscience, and thereby be once more deprived of their open access to God in worship. So, delicately, he suggests: 'Stay with me, for where I am conscience is no more a pain and already borders upon changing its nature to joy.'

We have seen that I Peter affords a bridge between the usage of Hebrews and that in the Pastoral Epistles[2]. The difference of emphasis between their respective handling of the interplay of *faith* with *conscience* is also interesting. The author of Hebrews would doubtless have subscribed to the opinion of the Pastorals concerning this[3]—but that is not his immediate concern. The meaning of *faith* for him in general is matter for a separate study: but when it appears in 10.22 it is as a part of that process of Christian initiation that has, as its negative fruit, the delivery from conscience, and thereby, as its positive, the bold entry *into the holy place*.[4]

---

[1] Cf. Heb. 13.20.   [2] See above, p. 97 f, on I Pet. 3.21.
[3] See above, p. 97.   [4] Heb. 10.19.

XII

NEW TESTAMENT, TAIL-PIECE
AND SUMMARY

SOME texts of the Fourth Gospel have preserved for us a late
Greek gloss explaining in terms of *conscience* the failure of the
scribes and the pharisees to continue their prosecution of the
woman taken in adultery.[1] Explanation is hardly necessary, but
the gloss offers an illuminating tail-piece to our search for the
meaning of *conscience* in the New Testament. It was written later
than any of the other occurrences which we have reviewed, by
one to whom Greek was his first, if not his only language. That
he uses it in the fullest MBA sense is significant confirmation of
the conclusions which we have reached and must shortly summarise.

The glossator adds to 'And they, when they heard it, went out
one by one . . .' the explanation 'being convicted in their own
conscience'.[2] The scribes and Pharisees have initiated a course
of action, twofold in its implications: they have haled the woman
off to stoning, and at the same time are regarding that cruel
penalty as quite incidental to their chief purpose, that of trapping
Jesus in his words. What Jesus says to them defeats the latter
intention and causes them to abandon the former; it also brings
into prominence not only their present course of action (but, of
course, initiated in the past), but also their unspecified past acts,
and their present condition arising from them. Conscience thus

---

[1] *The Adulteress Pericope* is not included by 'most of the ancient authorities' at
all, and those that do include it differ widely in their versions. It bears the marks
of a story authentic in origin even if wrongly placed here, and the variations do not
obscure its content but only add the comments which it may have gathered at
various times and places. The Received Text in including the gloss follows the late
uncials EGHKS of which the earliest is a sixth-century MS. Of the MSS. and
Versions which include the pericope, the gloss is omitted by DMUΓΛ of which
only Bezae is reasonably early. The Latin Versions as a whole contain no equivalent.
The absence of the gloss from any version subject to Latin influence justifies us in
taking it to be of Greek origin.   [2] John 8.9.

stirred from slumber so attacks them that they cannot complete their project.

All the elements of the final Pauline doctrine in Romans are here. There is the fixed moral law[1]: there is external judgment in the light of this law, not only on the woman[2] but also on her accusers.[3] In the case of the woman it bids fair to be executed through the temporal penalties inflicted by the society to which she belongs.[4] Her accusers, however, though no less sinners than she, are in no danger of such penalties–*the Wrath* mediated by human institutions. (That they are seeking to accuse Jesus shows that they have not escaped *the Wrath* mediated by nature,[5] but this is not stressed here.) They cannot, however, escape conscience: but this is no less an interpreter of the fixed moral Law, and no less a penalty, than *the Wrath*. They are convicted.[6]

The quickening of the conscience is here the work of the word of Christ[7] as it is later[8] to be that of the Holy Spirit who is only to come when He is departed[9]: it is quickened as a last resort–they have the Law, but they either ignore it to sin, or, worse, use it sinfully and for sinful ends. Society–in this case official Judaism–is powerless against them for *Wrath*; and thus they press on to transgress their fixed moral bounds, until they are brought up short by conscience. They know that what they are doing is wrong by direct experience within themselves: such *knowledge* is too painful for them to bear, and they 'went out one by one, beginning at the eldest even unto the last'.[10]

Before we summarise our findings there is one further appearance of συνείδησις in the N.T., discussion of which has been postponed until now. I Peter 2.19 is rendered by R.V.: 'For this is acceptable, if for conscience toward God a man endureth griefs, suffering wrongfully.'[11] That the alternative *of* for *toward* is suggested, in R.V. Margin, indicates clearly the justifiable hesitation felt by the translators in extracting *toward* from an unadorned genitive: while the meaninglessness of the sentence with *of* suggests that *conscience* is the wrong rendering here.

---

[1] John 8.5. [2] *Ibid.*, vv. 4 f, 11. [3] *Ibid.*, v. 7. [4] *Ibid.*, v. 5.
[5] *Ibid.*, v. 8, cf. Rom. 1.28.
[6] With the whole of this paragraph cf. pp. 68 ff, above, on Rom. 13.5.
[7] John 8.7. [8] *Ibid.*, 16.9.
[9] *Ibid.*, 7.39, cf. 15.26; 16.7, etc. For the juxtaposition of Christ and the Spirit with the MBA conscience see pp. 84 f above, on Rom. 9.1. [10] John 8.9.
[11] τοῦτο γὰρ χάρις, εἰ διὰ συνείδησιν Θεοῦ ὑποφέρει τις λύπας πάσχων ἀδίκως.

That this is so is borne out not only by the rest of the N.T. evidence but also by that of contemporary Greek popular usage as a whole. It goes without saying that throughout the N.T. the idea of God, holy and righteous, creator and judge, as well as redeemer and quickener, is the background against which *conscience* must be seen.[1] In three cases this background is for a moment, as it were, brought into focus, and the name of God[2] explicitly mentioned in connection with *conscience*; and in not one of them is the simple genitive used.[3] The use of the genitive in I Peter is thus without parallel in the N.T. if the English versions' rendering is right. But it is equally without parallel in the whole of Greek usage, in which, as we have already seen,[4] the genitive is consistently used with the substantives to stand for the object of σύνοιδα in the verbal phrase which they represent if they are to be rendered conscience.[5] Thus συνείδησίς τινος must be taken as equivalent to αὐτῷ τι συνειδέναι. But where the dative of the reflexive pronoun is so present the object of the phrase is always the act of its subject, whether completed or only initiated in the past, or the character or condition arising from the act. Thus αὐτῷ τι συνειδέναι always implies αὐτῷ τι πεπραχώς | πράξας | πράσσων συνειδέναι. In no way can *God* be conceived of as any man's own past act, least of all as a bad act, so that there is no need to point out again that in such a sentence the τι would, unless the reverse be explicitly stated, have to be taken to mean κακόν τι.[6] The best that can be done to justify the rendering *conscience* here, is to take Θεοῦ as a genitive of source, and paraphrase 'conscience is

---

[1] This is particularly true of the Pauline use proper; see pp. 67 ff above on Rom. 13.5.   [2] If it be legitimate to suppose that the N.T. is implicitly Trinitarian.
[3] In Acts 23.1, see p. 95 f, above, *God* is in the simple dative, the force of which, in connection with πεπολίτευμαι is to indicate that St. Paul's conduct is to be weighed as a member of God's people and nation. In Acts 24.16 πρὸς τὸν Θεόν means simply *in God's sight or presence* (cf. John 1.1). Although in II Cor. 4.2, συνείδησις is NA and cannot be rendered *conscience*, yet ἐνώπιον τοῦ Θεοῦ is only a variant of πρὸς τὸν Θεόν. For ἐν Χριστῷ and ἐν Πνεύματι Ἁγίῳ in Rom. 9.1, see above, pp. 84 f.   [4] P. 33, above.
[5] So he who, in Herodian IV.vii.1 (Ex 59), desired to quit Rome ὑπὸ τῆς τῶν ἔργων συνέσεως ἐλαυνόμενος was ὁ τὰ ἔργα αὐτῷ συνειδώς; cf. also Plutarch: *Quomodo quis suos in virtute sentiat profectus* 84D (Ex 50) cited below, p. 127; Democritus Fr. 297 (Diels)–Ex 72–cited above p. 34; Diod. Sic. iv.65 (Ex 78), cited above, p. 74, n. 3; Philo: Fr., ed. Mang II, p. 659 (Ex 79), cited above, p. 48; *Pap. BGU* IV.1024.iii.7 (Ex 88), cited above, p. 48, n. 7; also Plutarch: *Publicola* iv.99B (Ex 52), cited below, p. 115; Alciphron I.x.5 (Ex 38), cf p. 35, n. 3, above; Philodemus: *Rhet.* ii.140 (Ex 74); Dion. Halic.: *Ant.* viii.48.5 (Ex 77); Lucian: *Amores* 49 (Ex 80); *Pap. Oxy.* II.218ᵃ. ii.19 (Ex 82), etc.   [6] See pp. 24 ff, above.

God's agent: to suffer unjustly at the hands of men is to be preferred to suffering conscience (justly) at the hand of God'.[1] But such an interpretation is in itself hardly acceptable: it is plainly not the sense of the passage: it assumes an impossible degree of telescoping of meaning on the author's part: and it flies in the face of the evidence as to the current usages of the word.

Even were there evidence to support it, it is impossible to take the genitive as possessive here, thus representing the subject of σύνοιδα in the verbal phrase: for the passage would then ludicrously read 'for the sake of God's conscience' which can only mean 'in order to spare God the painful consciousness of His own past sin'.[2] The suggestion of a genitive of inner reference is also quite out of place here as is sufficiently demonstrated by the verbal gymnastics required to support such an interpretation.[3]

The most *recherché* exegesis really fails to make sense of the genitive here if συνείδησις means *conscience*. But the ingenuity that attempts it is misplaced. The genitive after συνείδησις is the object of σύνοιδα but that verb is not confined to use in the phrase αὐτῷ συνειδέναι. συνείδησις may often represent the simple σύνοιδα, and it plainly does so here. It is knowledge of God–and sure knowledge–that will enable a man to endure unjust suffering. But our experience of σύνοιδα compels us to ask the question: 'With whom is the knowledge shared?' When συνείδησις represents αὐτῷ συνειδέναι it is shared by a man with himself: in the absence of the reflexive pronoun, it is shared with another or others.[4] The context provides its own obvious answer. Although it is the *servants*[5] who are here specifically addressed, the charge is given to them as the first of three particular groups[6] within the 'elect race, the royal priesthood, the holy nation, the people for God's own possession'.[7] It is as members of the Church and not primarily as individuals that they have sure knowledge of God. This *knowledge* could not have so sufficient a reality as to uphold a man in face of unjust suffering, were it not fundamentally a *shared knowledge*.

The evidence which we have examined, then, enables us not

[1] Cf. pp. 67 ff, above on Rom. 13.5.   [2] Cf. p. 100, n. 4, above.
[3] Cf. Bengel cited by Selwyn, *The First Epistle of Peter* (p. 177), *ad loc.*
[4] See p. 29 f, above.   [5] I.e. οἰκέται, I Pet. 2.18.
[6] *Servants, ibid.,* 2.18; *Wives, ibid.,* 3.1; *Husbands, ibid.,* v. 7. Cf. *All* introduced by *Finally, ibid.,* v. 8.   [7] *Ibid.,* 2.9.

only entirely to agree with those commentators whose rendering of συνείδησις here is some variation on *awareness*,[1] but also to go further than they. The phrase means 'because you are Christians and as such share in the Church's sure knowledge of God'.

We have now examined every occurrence of συνείδησις in the N.T., in its context, in its relation to N.T. usage as a whole, and in the light of the popular Greek conception that underlies it. In summarising the results of our enquiry we can regard as certain that the N.T. writers not only took over the word *conscience* and its connotation complete from Greek popular thought but also left them in general as they found them. The differences in detail, significant though they are, are due not to alterations in the basic connotation, but to its being placed in a richer setting–that of the Judaeo-Christian doctrine of God, as Creator and sustainer of *all things*, righteous and holy. He judges men by the absolute moral standards inherent in his own nature, as it is revealed in the person of Christ Jesus. These standards are also mirrored in his works–that is, both in the nature of the creation as a whole, and in the nature of each of the myriad elements of which it is composed, not least, therefore, in the nature of man as a being capable of choice, and therein morally responsible.

Conscience in the New Testament, we may therefore summarise, is the painful reaction of man's nature, as morally responsible, against infringements of its created limits–past, present by virtue of initiation in the past, habitual or characteristic by virtue of frequent past infringements. It can be secondarily depicted as his capacity so to react, and this capacity in turn can be represented in terms of a near-personal metaphor. Because man's created nature as morally responsible is also rational, it can react wrongly: for wrong information can mislead. Environment also has considerable influence for good or ill; an environment which purveys a mistaken view as to the moral quality of certain acts, if it predispose a man to assume a right, or neutral, act to be wrong, will influence his nature to react against such right or neutral acts as if they were wrong, and *vice versa*. Habit, which is, of course, subject to the influence of environment, can also affect conscience: for habit can take on almost the force of the created

---

[1] E.g. Calvin, Alford, Westcott, Bigg, von Soden, Windisch and Wand: all *ad loc.* except Westcott on Heb. 9.9; as cited by Selwyn, *op. cit.*, p. 176.

limits themselves, so that breach of habit will frequently cause a reaction hardly to be distinguished from conscience, even where there is no moral significance. The trained soldier will 'have a conscience' if he desert his post under fire: the raw recruit will be quite undisturbed (till *the Wrath* overtake him), for to him it will have appeared the natural and sensible action. *Per contra*, habitual sin can so damage the limits of a man's nature that it no longer reacts when it should; until at last the stage is reached when a reaction akin to conscience is set up by good acts.[1] St. Paul would have granted that, for all its liability to error, conscience must be obeyed: but he would never have added 'for man has no other guide'.[2] He is definite that conscience only comes into play after at least the initiation of a wrong act; when it does not come into play, it may mean that the act committed is not wrong, but equally it may mean that the reactions are defective–either handicapped by wrong information, wrong environment or wrong habit, or made sluggish by sin, repeated and unrepented. In any case it can never mean that the action was more than 'not wrong'–that it was 'right' in the sense, even, of the only or best possible in the circumstances; still less can conscience have anything to say directly about future acts. There are many means by, and grounds on, which an assessment may be hazarded of the heat of bath water; the man's nature itself will not so react as to show whether it is too hot for him to get in, until he get in.

To some extent its fallible, and, to a far greater extent, its negative and *pis aller* character account for St. Paul's lack of enthusiasm for this Gentile experience, although he recognised it as valid, and good so far as it went. But Hebrews, preeminently, Acts and the Pastoral Epistles do not seriously misrepresent him when they suggest that the main reason for the minor place he allots it in his Christian scheme is, that, in Christ, having died to sin, a man should be free from conscience. He himself was forced to face the fact that the Christian did not automatically become

---

[1] Cf. Aristophanes: *Eq.* 184 (Ex 33) cited above, p. 45, for an ironical instance of the point made in I Tim. 1.19, 4.2 and Tit. 1.15 (*q.v.* pp. 92 ff, above); cf. also Isa. 5.20; Mark 3.20 ff and Matt. 6.23=Luke 11.35. But it is mistaken here to identify *the light* with conscience (cf. Thornton-Duesbery, *op. cit.*)–for conscience is but a small, and, because negative, the least significant, element in that *light*.

[2] H. D. Lewis, *Congregational Quarterly*, xxiv, p. 31. I owe this reference to Mr J. D. Walsh, Research Fellow of Magdalene College.

sinless at the moment of Baptism; but he did not think it a gross optimism to expect a Christian's behaviour to be, even when not ideal, at least sufficiently within the limits of his nature as created, to avoid the reaction that results from the attempt to exceed them. Later Christian experience may have had also to revise this expectation as still too optimistic—but not for a considerable time, and then with no little reluctance. But Hebrews would unquestionably have regarded 'a Christian suffering from conscience' to be a contradiction. Such a man had obviously fallen so far from the height, to which he had been raised by becoming a Christian, as to have fallen right out at the bottom, and to be back whence he had started; but with this significant difference, that the fall had broken his neck, so that he could never hope to rise again.[1] The distinction between *sin* and *sin unto death*,[2] which has led moral theologians into so many difficulties, seems to refer to just such a possibility as that contemplated in Hebrews. It is, therefore, possible that a closer study of the N.T. conception of *conscience* might have let in much light upon this vexed question. But that is not the present concern.

Lastly in this summary of the N.T. idea of *conscience*; it is closely involved with faith. Besides being, with repentance, man's own share in the divine-human work of Christian initiation—which work delivers man at last from conscience, for which there is no other remedy—faith is also that whereby conscience in the 'capacity' sense is quickened and informed. Conversely, outrages to conscience in this sense lead first to error concerning the faith, and, if persisted in without repentance, at last to its abandonment—to virtual 'de-initiation' as was seen above. The vicious circle is: 'error concerning the faith, leads to defective conscience-capacity, leads to worse error, etc.' History provides ample illustration of this principle—but it was derived by the N.T. writers from their conception of conscience. And it must be borne in mind that the same is true of all that has been said in the last eight chapters. Nothing has been got out of the word that was not either already in it when it reached the N.T. writers or, not so much put into it by them, as inferred from its existing content in the light of the faith that they held in common that 'Jesus is Lord' or 'the Christ is Jesus'.

[1] Cf. Heb. 6.1-6.   [2] I John 5.16 f.

XIII

CONSCIENCE IN THE
MODERN WORLD

OUR quest has now really reached its goal, so that the rest of this
book is no more than an epilogue, offering some observations on
the lines along which our findings may be found to be of relevance
to the pastoral situation of today. We have discovered conscience
in the N.T. to be the internal counterpart and complement of
the wrath. It is the painful consciousness that a man has of his
own sins, past or, if present, begun in the past.[1] It is *of God*[2] in
that it is the reaction of man's nature, as created, and so delimited,
by God, against moral transgressions of its bounds.[3]

The N.T. itself gives no indication as to the nature of the pain
of conscience. If, therefore, it is important to reach a description
of such pain, we must have recourse to the Greek popular usage
from which the word was adopted, and which provides ample
material for at least a tentative conclusion. When Xenophon
writes: 'I know that he thinks himself wronged by us; so that
when he sends for me I will not go–mainly because I am ashamed,
having on my conscience my utter deception of him; and also

---

[1] See above, pp. 43 ff, for non-N.T. usage, the analysis of which was found
applicable (p. 62 above) to the N.T. The exceptions to this generalisation in Greek
as a whole are rare. Of the six possible N.T. exceptions three are deceptive (II Cor.
4.2 and 5.11; I Pet. 2.19) as in them συνείδησις does not represent αὐτῷ συνειδέναι
but the simple συνειδέναι. Of the remainder only II Cor. 1.12 is certainly an exception, while Heb. 13.18 and I Pet. 3.16 are at most only partly so, and in any case
all three make it clear that they arise from the idea of *conscience* as so defined.

[2] The N.T. writers would only subscribe to the sentiment in Menander: *Monost.*
654 (Ex 66), cited above, p. 41, so long as θεός be rendered *divine (in origin)*. Conscience is not *God*, nor even *his voice in the soul*. It reflects and responds to the *Word
of God* whether 'understood by the things which are made' (Rom. 1.20), embodied
in the Torah, or incarnate in Jesus and thus active in the world through the Spirit;
but only within the limits of its function, viz. to turn man back from every attempt
to break out from the bounds imposed upon him by his Creator–'Hitherto shalt
thou come–but no further' (Job 38.11).

[3] There are of course also other, non-moral, transgressions which produce their
proper reaction. See above, p. 68 ff; cf. below p. 113.

because I am afraid lest he should take me and make suit against me in respect of those things in which he thinks himself wronged by me'[1]; he brings together what are the two dominant elements in conscience in Greek usage–*shame* and *fear*.[2] Thus Diogenes maintains that the greatest freedom from fear, and confidence, belong to the man with no evil on his conscience,[3] while Plato associates Alcibiades' conscience–his painful awareness that he abandons his good resolves for the sake of cheap popularity–with shame.[4] So, according to Demosthenes, the wrongdoer lives, as a result of conscience, the life of a hare, in fear and trembling, always looking for blows,[5] and Diphilus regards shame before the tribunal of his own conscience as the natural and proper reaction of a man to his past wrong acts.[6] We may therefore best summarise the pain of conscience as that combination of fear and shame which is called *guilt*–but not guilt legalistically conceived. The guilt which paralyses and *destroys*,[7] and is internally effective whether it be externally declared or not, is a phenomenon familiar to modern psychopathology.[8] It is only too rightly called a *disease*,[7] and he who suffers from it truly can never be called happy.[9]

If the pain of conscience is rightly so described, then it follows that it may produce physical symptoms: these will vary all but infinitely from person to person. Where they arise they will be the same for a given individual as those of either shame or fear, or both: but they are but symptoms, not the disease itself. That such symptoms may occur warns us of the danger, of misunderstanding the Bible, which lies in the attempt to partition off the

---

[1] Xen: *Anab.* I.iii.10 (Ex 24): ὅτι μέντοι ἀδικεῖσθαι νομίζει ὑφ' ἡμῶν οἶδα· ὥστε καὶ μεταπεμπομένου αὐτοῦ οὐκ ἐθέλω ἐλθεῖν, τὸ μὲν μέγιστον αἰσχυνόμενος, ὅτι σύνοιδα ἐμαυτῷ πάντα ἐψευσμένος αὐτόν, ἔπειτα καὶ δεδιὼς μὴ λαβών με δίκην ἐπιθῇ ὧν νομίζει ὑπ' ἐμοῦ ἠδικῆσθαι. The interplay of present and perfect tenses is illuminating.

[2] While it is true that Xenophon here isolates *shame* as the result of *conscience*, it is significant that in this juxtaposition of the internal and external causes of reluctance (i.e. *conscience* and *the Wrath*, in this case civil penalty, cf. pp. 67 ff, above, on Rom. 13.5) the former is τὸ μὲν μέγιστον.   [3] Diog. ap Stobaeus, *loc. cit.* (Ex 15).

[4] Plato: *Symp.* 216[b] (Ex 26).

[5] Dem: *de Corona* 263 (Ex 30).

[6] Diphilus ap Stobaeus, *loc. cit.* (Ex 31); cf. also Men: Fr. 632 (Kock) (Ex 34), cited above, p.25 ; Democritus: Fr. 297 (Diels) (Ex 72) cited above, p. 34; Philo: Fr. ed. Mang. II, p. 659 (Ex 79), cited above, p. 48; Bias ap Stobaeus, *loc. cit.* (Ex 68), cited above, p. 37, etc.

[7] Cf. Eur: *Or.* 395 f (Ex 17 and 56), cited above, p. 47.

[8] For a recent treatment from within Christianity see *Guilt* (Sheed and Ward, 1952) by F. C. Houselander, particularly the introduction.

[9] Cf. Xen: *Anab.* II.v.7 (Ex 21), cited above, p. 24.

various elements that go to the making of a man in his wholeness. Conscience is but one, the moral, of the reactions of the nature of a man as delimited by creation,[1] so that it needs to be emphasised that the illustrations which we have drawn from the physiological sphere are illustrations, and not analogies. They accord well with the outlook of the N.T. authors, for they were not inclined towards analysis of the human unity; for them, whatever metaphors they may employ, a man is a man, and it is the whole man that responds to the stimuli of the universe about him. Conscience is the reaction of the whole man to his own wrong acts. It is a moral reflex action, parallel, but also akin, to those reactions that make a man drop a red hot poker or spew out a poison, long before conscious reasoning has been brought to bear on those objects. The absolute pitch of the trained musician is likewise akin to the moral 'absolute pitch' of the trained Christian: the wrong note—be it never so little wrong—causes immediate pain.

We have seen that St. Paul introduced *conscience* into Christianity; and in this epilogue it will be assumed that it is his authority which gives it whatever standing it has therein, and that therefore his view of it should be taken as the norm. He does not, however, claim it as a part of revelation, but merely accepts it as a universal experience among men and admits its—limited—validity. In the nature of the case it is impossible to prove this universality, and each individual can only test such an assertion by introspection. Some external indications of its probability are available. We have already seen that the notion was at any rate current coin in the Greek world, and shall see that the Latin world knew of it also.[2] Later European language and literature is so influenced by Christianity that nothing can be argued from it; but some corroboration is afforded from beyond the bounds of both Christianity and even the Indo-European languages. The Burmese have no word for *conscience* but when they wish to say *he has no conscience* they say *shame-fear is not* or *he has not shame-fear*.[3]

---

[1] See above, pp. 67 ff, on Rom. 13.5.
[2] They did not however confine *conscientia* exclusively to its description; see below, p. 118 f.
[3] I owe this statement to the Rev. Canon G. L. Tidey, formerly Warden of Holy Cross College, Rangoon, who quotes his Burmese Sub-Warden. Canon Tidey

H

In any case, whatever view be taken of the authority of the Pauline conception of *conscience* for Christianity, or of his rightness in assuming it, with the Greek world from which he adopted it, to be an experience common to man as man,[1] one thing is immediately obvious. The definition which we have reached of *conscience* in the N.T. is very different from any that might be abstracted from modern English usage of the word, not only in popular speech but also by technical writers on ethics, including Christian ethics.

It is not the intention of this study to offer a critique of various popular and technical doctrines of the nature of conscience, but only to arrive, by collection and analysis of the data, at a conclusion both as to the Greek popular usage inherited by the N.T., and as to the N.T. usage itself, and to allow that conclusion to provide its own critique. Let us now therefore take the following admirable and scholarly example of a modern description of *conscience* as typical of all, while more comprehensive than most. It takes into account the opinions of theologians, moralists and psychologists, as well as the popular notion, and sets them against a background of the teaching of the (Western) Church. If the definition of conscience as 'that tendency of human nature which leads both conative and cognitive elements to seek unsparingly for satisfaction in the good, the beautiful, the true'[2] be juxtaposed with the definition which we have reached, the disparity between them is manifest. For the sake of brevity the contrast can be effectively pointed by reference to the three focal points of our definition.

'The orthodox view', says Bertrand Russell,[3] 'is that wherever two courses of action are possible, conscience tells me which is right, and to choose the other is sin.' Whether or not this be really the orthodox view is irrelevant: what is significant is that an author of such calibre should gain the impression that it is. But *conscience* in Greek, and the N.T. offers no exception to this, does not look to the future: its reference is to acts at least begun, if not irrevocably completed, in the past. It tells me that what I have done is sin: whether its absence can be taken to tell me that

adds: 'I have never heard any Buddhist using *conscience* in the way that we use it'–i.e. the modern English popular usage–'it is much too difficult for simple villagers.'

[1] See above, p. 40 f.
[2] K. E. Kirk: *Some Principles of Moral Theology*, Cap. viii, p. 177.
[3] *History of Western Philosophy*, p. 200.

what I have done is righteousness, may be thought debatable despite the evidence presented in this essay, but there is no question about the tense of the action referred to. Russell's claim however that he is stating the orthodox view does not lack support from Christian writers[1]: that his is in any case the popular notion is evidenced abundantly by popular literature which makes such statements as: 'His conscience told him that his peculiar position at this critical moment entailed certain duties towards the deceased.'[2] If here the conscience is conceived of as *advising* about future acts, other examples show it as compelling to them. Thus 'in a cruel and unenlightened age one has to be cruel and unenlightened in order to survive–or even in order to accomplish the good deeds to which one's conscience urges one'.[3] Conscience as compelling to action is found, it is true, many times in Greek usage: but it is always the painful consciousness of a past wrong act compelling to such action as it is hoped may remove or at least relieve the pain.[4]

The word συνείδησις wherever it is to be rendered *conscience*, represents αὑτῷ συνειδέναι. It thus refers to a man's own acts or to his own character arising from or expressed in those acts. Although, therefore, St. Paul in I Corinthians speaks strongly against any behaviour which might lead others to run the risk of suffering conscience by following such an example, yet conscience cannot be thought of as having any right to pass judgment on another's acts, still less on his opinions.[5] It is, then, far from employing the word in its N.T. sense to say that the moral teaching and character even of Jesus himself must await the approval of the conscience (of the individual). It is no more than pressing this notion to its only possible conclusion to continue with the assertion that 'the conscience ought to prevail against the *ipse dixit* of any authority, however justly venerated (including Christ)'.[6] That here *collective* is added to *conscience* mitigates the

---

[1] Cf. for example Kirk, *op. cit.*, p. 177, para 2, who supports it by adding *contemplated* even when discussing what he labels *the narrower sense of the word*.

[2] T. L. Phipson: *The Storm and its Portents*, p. 10.

[3] Stephen Williams, in *The Radio Times*, 21 Dec. 1951.

[4] Cf. Plutarch: *Publicola* iv.99ᴮ (Ex 52): ἐλαυνόμενος τῷ συνειδότι τοῦ πράγματος, ὥρμησε . . .; although the context shows that here the content is not really the πρᾶγμα but keeping silent about it. Cf. also Plutarch: *De sera numinis vindicta* 556ᴬ (Ex 51), cited above, p. 34; and Herodian IV.vii.1 (Ex 59), cited above, p. 106.

[5] See above, pp. 77 f, on I Cor. 10.29 f.

[6] Hastings Rashdall: *Conscience and Christ*, p. 30.

strangeness of this dictum: but it removes *conscience* one stage further from its N.T. roots. Still further from those roots–for the N.T., like Greek folk-wisdom, regarded the *conscience* as an experience common to man as man[1]–is the notion, of the trained professional wielder of conscience as a judge of others, inherent in the judgment that 'to say what is the present value of Our Lord's teaching is the business of the philosopher or of the moralist'.[2]

Whether the man-in-the-street shares, consciously or unconsciously, these views held by professional moralists is not easy to demonstrate.[3] They are, however, certainly shared by at least one who claims to be a 'Man of the World'.[4] He starts from the conception of conscience as *the guide of God in every heart*, and as the complement of common sense, which is the *guide of God in every brain*; and comes, by way of the axiom that *conscience and common sense create religion*, to the conclusion that 'until the divinity of Christ is acknowledged by all to have been superimposed by men, nothing can be done' to provide a sensible religion and ethic. It is alarming, but perhaps not surprising to discover that, for this writer, *common sense* is simply what any man might suppose to be the truth without any knowledge of the relevant facts, and that *conscience* is called in to lend the appearance of some religious validity.

It is not without interest that while in the book *Conscience and Common Sense*, *Conscience* is but a poor second best, in the book *Conscience and Christ* it is Christ who is a poor second best. But in the latter work *conscience* is held to be *moral consciousness*–that is, an activity of the human mind. But if this is to be not confined to specialists but a universal attribute, it is virtually the same thing as *common sense*. It is, therefore, doing neither writer an injustice to define this as *uninformed opinion* with the addition of perhaps a few facts and authoritative judgments selected in the light of that opinion.[5]

[1] See above, pp. 40 f and 113 f.   [2] *Op. cit.*, p. 62.   [3] But see below, pp. 122, 125 f.
[4] *Conscience and Common Sense* by 'a Man of the World', privately published by Hatchard, 1911. In fairness it must be admitted that both the form and the content of this curious work tend to suggest that the author, whoever he was, was perhaps a little eccentric; nevertheless he is at pains to point out that he is an Etonian and a Magistrate; and pastoral experience might well support his claim to the title 'a Man of the World'; see further below, pp. 122, 125.
[5] I.e. by the process described in the psychological term *rationalisation*.

We need look at no further examples to see how far the modern notion of conscience has drifted from that of the N.T. in the third main aspect. Those already quoted–and they are typical–show that modern English usage regards conscience as a guide to future action independent of and superior to any other such guide, and to the counsel or command of any authority whatever. It can therefore be claimed as sufficient justification of a course of action adopted or contemplated, or opinion held, even although no facts are taken into account and all authority is defied. The New Testament, however, emphatically denies this: conscience is the *subsequent* pain which indicates that sin has been committed by the man who suffers it. Where there is no conscience its absence cannot be taken as more than some corroboration of the hope, reached mainly on other grounds, that the action in question was right. 'I do not know whether what I did was right or not: I have not sufficient knowledge. But at least it has not awakened the pain of conscience: that is something to be said for my course of action, but is far less than justification of it' is the Pauline summary.[1]

Conscience, then, is taken today as justifying, in advance or in general principle, actions or attitudes of others as well as one's self. But in the New Testament it cannot justify; it refers only to the past and particular; and to the acts of a man's own self alone.

A quite separate study would be required to trace this decline from the N.T. conception of *conscience* into that current today, whether in theological thought[2] or in popular expression,[3] and to discover its causes. Some suggestions have been advanced as they arose in the study of the N.T. but these will not be pursued: now we need only posit what seems most likely to have been the first step in the decline.

When we examined *the Adulteress Pericope* we saw that the 'conscience gloss' was confined, among those MSS. that include the *Pericope*, to the exclusively Greek texts: no Latin version contains it, and the usage is an apt summary of the N.T. conception.[4] There is here a hint–it falls far short of proof–that the

[1] See above, pp. 88 ff, on I Cor. 4.4.
[2] As summarised by Kirk, *op. cit.*, see p. 114, above.
[3] As illustrated above, pp. 114 ff.
[4] See p. 104 f, above, on John 8.9.

first step in the decline coincides with the first translation of the Greek original into a Latin version. *Conscientia* was the obvious word to use, and yet its use was fatal.

The briefest glance at any Latin Dictionary or Thesaurus shows at once that while *conscientia* can be used exactly in accordance with the MBNorm usage of συνείδησις, nor are examples of usage similar to the Greek MBA lacking, yet in the case of the Latin word it is not the norm. In Greek, as was seen, MA was always MBA; but this is far from the case in Latin, in which *conscientia* could be used absolutely to mean either *a good conscience* (in the modern sense)[1] or *a bad conscience*[2] quite indifferently. Further the word is far from being appropriated to a moral context to anything approaching the extent to which συνείδησις was in Greek in general, and in the N.T. in particular. In brief it may be fairly said that *conscientia* includes the meaning of συνείδησις in its Greek and N.T. connotation, but includes so much more besides, as to fail completely to exclude the modern notion of conscience. Its use in translation, therefore, could not fail to reduce what was for the N.T. writers a precise, indeed somewhat narrow, idea, into a conception so broad, vague and formless as to confuse rather than clarify all ethical discussion from that moment forward.

It is of particular significance that the word is very common in the Latin Stoic writers. Cicero who, although an eclectic, was inclined in moral questions to accept the teaching of Stoicism: Varro, whose views were most akin to Stoicism, and of whom Cicero so strongly approved: Virgil, who includes Stoic ideas in his blend of animistic folk-lore with philosophy: Pliny, who studied under Epictetus' teacher Musonius: and perhaps above all Seneca; all made frequent use of the word, in other senses, however, as well as that of an ethical norm. The influence of at least the first two on the Latin fathers, and particularly on St. Augustine is well-known, and it is probable that there is no need to seek further than the writings of these and of Seneca for the source of the idea of a Stoic origin for συνείδησις that has vitiated exegesis of the N.T. connotation of that word.[3]

It may with some plausibility be advanced that the most com-

---

[1] E.g. Cic: *Att*. XII.xxviii.2.   [2] *Ibid., Rosc. Am.* xxiv.67.
[3] Cf. Cap i above.

prehensive single rendering of *conscientia* in English would be *common sense*: for all writers agree that whatever it may mean it is something common to man as man. The Latin tradition of *conscience* would thus be of *common sense as applied to moral questions*, and so very close, as has been seen, to today's usage, both technical and popular.[1]

[1] Cf. above, pp. 114 ff, and below, p. 129 f.

XIV

CONSCIENCE AND THE CHURCH

IF our treatment of *conscientia* in the last chapter is very cursory, it is because the reasons for the disparity between the modern English, and the N.T., *conceptions* of conscience are hardly of major importance. The really significant thing is that this disparity exists, and the important question is: 'Does it matter?'

Christian Theology can never afford to ignore that question: for to do so is to forget that ultimately it is but the handmaid of the pastoral ministry. Its concern must always be to contribute, however remotely and however little, to the helping of ordinary men and women in the living of Christian lives, and towards the full appropriation of the benefits of Christ's passion. St. Paul rightly saw that it was the duty of those with *knowledge*, so far from placing *stumbling-blocks* in the way of the *little ones*, to remove them.[1] It is with an assertion that, in so far as it differs from and distorts the New Testament conception, the modern notion of conscience is just such a *stumbling-block*, that we bring this study to its conclusion.

The apparent obsession with idolatry, as the prime cause of whatever might ail Israel, politically, militarily or 'ecclesiastically', which is a mark of the forerunners of Our Lord, is not mistaken, nor is it primitive or outmoded. The underlying assumption is sound: that man is never without a religion, will always be worshipping somebody or something, and that his life will pivot upon that worship and religion: and that for this worship there is but one proper object, the Living and the True God. Any other object—however divine in origin, however good in its proper place, be it even 'the holiest creature that ever God made'[2]—once worship is misdirected to it, and away from God, becomes an

---

[1] I Cor. 8 and 10.23 ff; Rom 14.13 ff.
[2] Cf. *The Cloud of Unknowing, ed.* Underhill, heading to Chapter VI.

abomination. When made the focus of religion, it can only seduce men from their proper worship–in which alone they may find redemption and fulfilment–and thus misshape their lives.

The apostles and the N.T. writers are in complete agreement with their predecessors in this. If the O.T. looked for the cause of Israel's distress in their having turned aside from the living God to the worship of *dumb idols*, the N.T. calls *good news* that which caused men to reverse this process.[1]

The modern pastor might therefore not be unwise to observe the same principle in seeking to determine the cause of the present condition of Christian faith, practice and worship. Whatever signs of revival may be observable at the present time, there can be no question that such religious observance as would have been recognised by the Apostles and their contemporary Christians as in any degree Christian is, in England at any rate, confined to a minority. On the Biblical assumption the rest will have some other religion, must be worshipping some object, so that the principle *Cherchez l'idole* can therefore be applied with profit.

There are doubtless many such 'idols' that can be discovered if this term be taken to indicate whatever seduces from the worship of God, and much homiletic is validly based on such an interpretation. But the true requirement of such an 'idol' as is now sought is that those who offer to it the worship, veneration and heed that properly belong to God alone should really suppose themselves, by their cult of this object, to be fulfilling their religious obligations. Sin seduces from the worship of God; although all men are to some extent seduced by it, those who make it their religion are exceptional, and in any case they do not suppose it to be 'the Christian religion'–for, in England at any rate, the Christian religion dies sufficiently hard for *religion* normally to connote in the popular mind some form of Christianity.

There are those who, at this stage, will, according to their convictions or dispositions, cry 'Mariolatry', 'Bibliolatry', 'Mysteriolatry', 'Ecclesiolatry', or some such thing. These, it would be argued, have in common that each takes a valid element or elements, more or less essential, in the Christian religion and so distorts it, or its place in the whole, as to vitiate true Christian worship. But neither they nor any similar 'idolatry', nor even

[1] Cf. I Thess. 1.9; Acts 14.15; I Cor. 12.2; Gal. 4.8 ff and *passim.*

idolatry in the literal sense, fulfil the essential requirement of that
'idolatry' now sought. For none of them, however bad or mistaken they may be held to be, seduces the would-be Christian
from that basic minimum overt act recognised in Primitive
Christianity and now most readily summed up in the jejune
phrase, *church-going*. The 'idol' now sought must, like these, be a
valid element in the Christian religion, of apparently irreproachable authority, but such that those who venerate it and identify it
with the real object of worship will abandon church-going, and
even lesser but kindred activities such as private devotions and
Bible-reading, while retaining the conviction that they are prac-
tising Christians, and claiming for themselves that name.

Even were we attempting more than an epilogue at this stage,
in the nature of the case evidence would be awkward to introduce:
so that it must suffice to assert that the pastoral ministry intensively
and analytically pursued provides ample evidence to suggest that
conscience–in the modern sense–is the 'idol' that we are seeking.
Menander declared that the universal experience of conscience
was divine[1]; if by this he meant *divine in origin* St. Paul himself
would not have disagreed. But he, and the whole N.T., disagrees
radically with modern man when he goes further and says 'Conscience is God–in every man', while so understanding *conscience*
as to go on to infer that no man therefore has any need of Bible,
Church, Ministry, Creeds, Sacraments, worship or devotion. He
has God in him, and the whole of Christianity can be summed up
by *conscientia semper sequenda*.

This last phrase is not, of course, the invention of modern
popular thought: it was 'not merely introduced but maintained
throughout as her crowning moral doctrine'[2] by Christianity. We
have already seen that St. Paul, who introduced *conscience* into
Christianity, did so under compulsion,[3] and was very far from
regarding it as his 'crowning moral doctrine'. But, that apart,
the doctrine would be quite unexceptionable were *conscience* to be
understood in the New Testament sense, in which case the phrase
would mean: 'When what you are doing awakes conscience you
must stop: when the act is already complete you must repent–or
risk losing all that was given you in Baptism.' But no more is

---

[1] *Monost.* 654 (Ex 66), cited above, p. 41; cf. also p. 111, n. 2.
[2] K. E. Kirk: *Conscience and its Problems*, p. 60.   [3] Above, p. 64 ff.

the idea that 'conscience is (the voice of) God' in every man the invention of modern popular thought[1]: this too is no less unexceptionable in the N.T. sense of the word: it merely adds to the paraphrase above: '. . . for conscience is the reaction of your nature as created by God against your transgression of the limits He set to it. It is thus the action of God, mediated by your nature, to warn you to stop.'

The word and idea as used and understood by N.T. authors is ill-adapted by virtue of its severe limitation to adoption as an 'idol'. It is perhaps conceivable that it might have been so adopted: but it remains that it never was. In its modern sense, however, it provides an 'idol' that could hardly be bettered. *Corruptio optimi pessima*: properly understood and thus properly safeguarded the conscience can justly be described in these strong terms: once let it escape its N.T. limitations, and the more shades of meaning it gathers, while still retaining its high authority, the more diabolical an *abomination* does it become, at the last offering 'authoritative' justification for the abandonment of the basic minimum of Christian religious observance.

The pastor, therefore, that is, the teaching Church, has no one but himself to blame if the *little ones* have stumbled and continue to stumble, away from everything in Christianity that smacks, however slightly, of the theological or the institutional, till the name of Christian can only be applied to them by a gross extension of its primitive sense. He has taken a human experience and raised it to the skies, calling its name 'the most important of moral terms, the crowning triumph of ethical nomenclature', and describing it as 'the internal, absolute, supreme judge of individual action'.[2] He has then offered it to his flock, while telling them nothing of its nature; nothing of its limitations; nothing, in fact, of the very precise connotation it had in the mind of him who alone authorised its introduction into Christianity, and in imitation of whom it was used by other N.T. authors.

There can be small wonder at the result so penetratingly described by Daubeny.[3] 'Dreadful consequences are derivable to society . . . (from the use of) . . . a plausible word wrested from

---

[1] Cf. Bonaventura, Sent. ii.d.39, a.1, q.3, ad 3; cited by Kirk, *op. cit.*, p. 53.

[2] J. B. Lightfoot: *Saint Paul's Epistle to the Philippians*, excursus; *St. Paul and Seneca*.

[3] *Guide to the Church*, 1798. I owe this reference to Mr J. D. Walsh, Research Fellow of Magdalene College.

its proper sense.' 'It has been imagined that provided men follow the directions of their own "consciences" they are justified in whatever mode of conduct they may adopt, which (as the term "conscience" is now too generally understood) is . . . in other words to say that because men are persuaded a thing is right therefore it cannot be wrong.'

'Conscience'–or should it rather be called 'private persuasion'– is 'therefore considered as the private judgment of the party on the legality or illegality of his own conduct.' 'When men therefore talk of "liberty of conscience" they would do well to consider whether it is not, as the phrase is now generally understood, rather a liberty of their own making than any portion of that liberty with which Christ has made them free.'

The Church is nevertheless right, and has the duty, to teach that Conscience is inviolable; that any action must be stopped or, if too late, repented, if it has awoken conscience. Nor would any authority be justified in overruling it in this sense. But to allow men to suppose it infallible, while understanding it in a sense wider to a ludicrous degree than any it has in the N.T. is as great a disservice to them as can be imagined. It is nothing less than a complete abdication of the office to which she is appointed. She who is commissioned to proclaim to men the self-revelation of the One God, Creator and Lawgiver, King and Father; she whose first creed was 'Jesus is Lord'; she upon whom the Holy Spirit rests with power, whose Apostles can assert that they 'too have the Spirit of God'[1] and can tell the most refractory *little ones* that they 'have the mind of Christ'[2]; she who has not only the power but the duty to bind and loose on earth[3]; is in these last days content to abandon her children to a 'nursemaid'[4] only authorised to act when all else has failed and they are rushing headlong into disaster, and then not with advice, counsel or guidance, but only with deterrent pain.

This is what she in fact does whensoever she offers men no better guidance than 'act according to conscience'[5] for this is the

---

[1] I Cor. 7.40.   [2] I Cor. 2.16.   [3] Cf. Matt. 16.19, 18.18.
[4] Cf. Epict: Fr. 97 (Schweighaüser) (Ex 54 and 84) above, pp. 51 ff.
[5] For a very recent instance of this cf. *Infallible Fallacies* (SPCK 1953) p. 30, l. 36 ff. This is not an *ex cathedra* pronouncement, no doubt; but it was commended to 'our people' by the Archbishop of Canterbury in his Presidential Address to the Convocation of Canterbury, 14 Oct. 1953.

meaning with which *conscience* was authoritatively introduced into Christianity. But that is not the sole measure of her abdication. Not only does she permit her children to suppose that conscience is a sufficient guide in all things, but by doing so without clearly defining conscience, she subscribes, in effect, to the popular 'wresting from its proper sense' of the word, and countenances the interpretation of the word that men are only too ready to put upon it.

For when modern man says 'My conscience bids me to do this' he means one of three things, or any blend in any proportions of two or more of them. These three are:

(1) (Reason)	'I	{ have decided / think it is right / think I ought }	to do this'
(2) (Emotion)	'I	{ want to do / feel like doing }	this'
(3) (Habit)		'I am by environment and habit so conditioned that this is the natural, instinctive, and, therefore, least troublesome action for me to take.'	

The blends are obvious: both opinions and inclinations are subject to the influence of environment and habit: inclinations can readily be rationalised, and reason clouded by desire or circumstances. To call any of these, still more any blend of these, *infallible* or even *inviolable* is bad enough even if, *per impossibile*, they be considered absolutely. When they are seen against the background of secular or even heathen environment or habit, corrupt desires, and a reason that, even if it has, on occasion, all the relevant facts at its disposal, still remains fallen, then for such an estimate, the description 'abomination' bids fair to shed its inverted commas.

Man must think out and decide how he is going to act: he must act from the heart: and he must acquire habits–he can avoid doing so no more than he can live apart from any environment. But to call any one, or any blend, of these, *conscience*, and thereby to allow men to suppose that the acts to which they prompt are *infallibly*, or *inviolably*, right (or at least *sequenda*), is woefully to mislead and in any case utterly to distort the conception of the

N.T. Nor is it excessive to say that *the Wrath* is sufficiently in evidence, as the result of this 'idolatry' and its condonation, to validate these assertions.

Although, then, these three sources of decision, separately or in any combination, have a vital part to play in Christian, and indeed in all human ethics, the N.T. will not permit us to call them *conscience*. To our obvious questions 'What then shall we call them and what is their relation to conscience?', while the N.T. itself does not reply, the Greek world from which *conscience* was adopted offers a hint at a satisfactory answer. Greek popular usage employs on occasion the word προαίρεσις[1] as complementary to but contrasted with conscience. This word we shall translate as *choice*, and it is of this, and not of conscience, that the three elements which we analysed[2] are factors. They are, if not a man's lights, at least the lenses through which those lights must enter his perception in order to effect action.

At this stage it would be out of place to embark upon a detailed dissertation on ascetical theology: but once the N.T. conception of conscience has been defined it becomes plain that the primary concern of the Church in the sphere of ethics[3] must be the education of these two complementary elements. *Choice* is prior, and *Conscience*, if it arise at all, subsequent, to action. Where there is no choice there can be no conscience, although there may well be a parallel experience: for only where there is

---

[1] In line 9 of *Pap. BGU*, IV.1024.iii.7 (Ex 88) of which lines 5-7 have been cited above, p. 48, n. 9, this word appears as complementary to and contrasted with the συνείδησις of line 7. The relationship is more clearly seen in *Arch. Pap.* iii.418.13 (Ex 70). That this is probably a set formula for oaths seems most probable from its close similarity to *Pap. Par.* II.15 (Ex 71) which is best shown by citing them in parallel, and underlining the common elements.

Arch. Pap. iii.418.13 (Ex 70)	*Pap. Par.* 21.15 (Ex 71)
ἑκουσίᾳ γνώμῃ καὶ αὐθαιρέτῳ βουλήσει καὶ ἀμετανοήτῳ καὶ ἀδόλῳ προαιρέσει βεβαίᾳ συνειδήσει ὀρθῇ διανοίᾳ δίχα παντὸς δόλου καὶ φόβου καὶ βίας καὶ ἀπάτης καὶ ἀνάγκης καὶ περιγραφῆς πάσης καὶ συναρπαγῆς ... ⟨ὁμολογοῦμεν⟩	ὁμολογοῦμεν γνώμῃ ἑκουσίᾳ καὶ αὐθαιρέτῳ βουλήσει καὶ ἀδόλῳ συνειδήσει καὶ ἀμετατρέπτῳ λογισμῷ καὶ ἀμετανοήτῳ προαιρέσει ...

All these examples are, it is true, very late but the popular provenance of the latter two seems unquestionable. The dividing line between popular asseveration and legal formulary is very faint; cf. 'So help me God' in current English slang as 'Swelp me!'; see also p. 37, above, n. 3.   [2] P. 125.

[3] We must remember that, in the N.T., any legal code is as much a *pis aller*, a nursemaid, as conscience itself. (Cf. Gal. 3.23 ff, etc.) The production of such a code, although it may be forced on the Church, is so far from being her primary concern as to be a counsel of despair.

choice has an act any moral quality. Where the choice is right, or at least not wrong, there will be no conscience either. Where there is conscience the choice was wrong, the action must be abandoned and the choice revised. Conscience can refute choice: which is thus yet another indication that choice is not only fallible, but violable as well–for conscience having refuted, the agent must violate it. But conscience–although fallible–is the last ditch and must not be violated. While being distinct, therefore, these two operate in such close co-operation that they may well be educated together. There are other reasons also to recommend this. Thus while reason must perhaps on earth ever remain fallen, it will function better in proportion as the information on which it has to work is accurate. Desire or inclination, while liable to terrible corruptions if misdirected, have few equals as a force for good if they be but provided with worthy objects: and environment can be changed, and habits thereby altered in adaptation to it. But conscience we have seen to depend to some extent for its accuracy upon accurate information[1], and to be partly conditioned by environment and habit.[2] As to desire, the Greek world was well aware that there are few awakeners of conscience more potent than the gulf between aspiration and achievement, if the aspiration be sufficiently exalted for a gulf to be apparent.

'He who would truly make progress (in virtue) ought not simply to have his heart turned and tears started by the sermons of the philosopher: he should rather see himself in comparison with the works and behaviour of the good and perfect man. Then at the same time as he is gnawed by conscience at his falling-short (of such a standard), he will have joy through hope and desire, and will be full of a striving that is never still, as he yearns all but to be made one with the good man.'[3] This most impressive and inspiring pronouncement lacks only two normative features of the N.T. It would be as succinct and satisfying a summary of the authentic Christian ethic as could be desired, did

[1] Pp. 77, 83, above. [2] P. 83, above.
[3] Plutarch: *Quomodo quis suos in virtute sentiat profectus* 84D (Ex 50): οὐ γὰρ ὑπὸ τῶν λόγων δεῖ τοῦ φιλοσοφοῦντος μόνον τὴν καρδίαν στρέφεσθαι καὶ δάκρυα ἐκπίπτειν, ἀλλ' ὅ γε προκόπτων ἀληθῶς, μᾶλλον ἔργοις καὶ πράξεσιν ἀνδρὸς ἀγαθοῦ καὶ τελείου παραβάλλων ἑαυτόν, ἅμα τῷ συνειδότι τοῦ ἐνδεοῦς δακνόμενος καὶ δι' ἐλπίδα καὶ πόθον χαίρων καὶ μεστὸς ὢν ὁρμῆς οὐκ ἠρεμούσης τῷ ἀγαθῷ μονονουχὶ συμφῦναι γλιχόμενος.

it but take knowledge of *faith*, and realise that only in Christ is such a *good and perfect man* to be found: all the other features are there. The N.T. writers might well have omitted the *all but*, and have preferred *love* to *desire*.[1] The *turning* of the *heart* strikes the true note of prophecy. Due attention is paid to *works*, and an external standard of *comparison* as well as object of aspiration, is insisted on. There is *hope, love, joy, ceaseless striving*–'running with patience the race that is set before us'.[2] In this rich complex, however, we must notice that conscience is but one element, and far from the whole. Its function is solely to make the man painfully aware of the gulf between aspiration and achievement.

For the training, therefore, of choice and conscience the Church has five main duties, and has been supplied with the resources for performing them.

(*a*) She must make of herself the best possible environment. The evaporation of the idea of the Church as a society to which a man belongs, and in which he has a responsible part to play, into an idea of it as a building which he visits from time to time and from which he receives something, cannot but weaken the effectiveness of the Church in this part of her task.

(*b*) She must, as far as possible, so influence the secular environment in which she and her members have to live that it is as little inimical as may be to her purpose.

(*c*) She must set before her members, and anyone else who will listen, the relevant facts: these include not only, although primarily, the great truths of revelation, and the beliefs dependent on them which are 'necessary to salvation'; but also the facts of her own experience–being the sum of that of her countless members. It must be remembered that, for the individual, attacks of conscience, consequent upon earlier choices and action, become relevant factors in subsequent choices: only to a less degree is this true for the Church as a whole. She must take into account, and maintain as a relevant fact, the occurrence of conscience, after a given act, to but one, and he the least, of her *little ones*.

(*d*) She must set forth the historical life of Christ as the pattern to be emulated, and his teaching as commentary upon it, in such a way that it may be effective as the object of aspiration no less

---

[1] I.e. ἀγάπη to πόθος, but the latter is used here in a purged and rarefied sense.
[2] Heb. 12.1.

than attractive, together with the ultimate rewards to which it leads, as the object of desire *par excellence*.

(*e*) Habit is formed partly by environment, partly by choice, and there is constant interplay between the three. Much of the Church's task in the cultivation of right habit will have been done by the faithful fulfilment, therefore, of the duties (*a*)–(*d*) above. But criticism of action is also necessary if there is to be progress, as well as avoidance of bad habit. Conscience as critic of action will at most say that it is 'not wrong'. The Church must, therefore, bring to bear on the question of wherein it might have been better, the unique accumulation of 1900 years of conscious ethical experience.

To these five elements in the training of choice and conscience together, a sixth must be added concerned with conscience alone. We have seen that the capacity for it can be so deadened that the conscience will never awake at all, or will awake wrongly[1]; and also that, *per contra*, it can be sharpened.[2] Perhaps the fullest fruit of Christian asceticism is a moral sensitivity so acute, a narrowing of the limits within which conscience-free action is possible to so fine a degree, that conscience would not only arise at the smallest deviation from Christian perfection, but also even at the prior imaginative contemplation of such deviation. No doubt this could only be so in Christ himself: the greatest of the Saints by their own confession fall far short of it. The world will sneer at even the smallest beginnings of such an achievement –a sort of moral absolute pitch[2]–as 'scrupulosity'. But the Christian should never be afraid of having scruples, but only of having the wrong scruples.

If, in the light of a true understanding of the N.T. conception of conscience, the ethical function of the Church must be formulated along some such lines as these, then it is plain that in the practical exercise of this vital element of the Church's ministry–in every other field the office of certain authorised representatives set apart by whatever means from among her members–there is a far larger place than is often allowed for the learned director of souls.[3] To leave men to 'conscience' is in effect to leave them

---

[1] Above, p. 109, n. 1.   [2] Above, p. 113.

[3] The substance of this comment was made, in conversation on this book when it was only projected, by the Bishop of Durham, Dr A. M. Ramsey, when Regius Professor of Divinity at Cambridge.

I

without the assistance they have a right to expect in the determining of action. Such an abandonment supposes choice to be an aspect of conscience and to be, therefore, equally infallible or at least inviolable with it: whereas they are in fact quite distinct and the former is as fallible and violable as any other activity of man. With all the help that revelation, the experience of the Church, and Grace in all its operations can provide, moral choice still can never entirely escape being a 'shot in the dark'. If the Church withhold all such help then 'how great is that darkness'.[1]

[1] Matt. 6.23.

ANALYTICAL INDEX
OF GREEK SOURCES

A. The Verbal Phrase

αὑτῷ συνειδέναι

I	II	III	IV	V
SERIAL No.	REFERENCE TO SOURCE	APPROX. DATE FL.	REF. TO PAGE	CONTENT OF αὑτῷ συν-ειδέναι—I.E. PARTICIPLE, ABSTRACT NOUN OR EQUIV.
1	Plato: *Apol.* 21[b]	400 B.C.	22	*being wise*
2	Plato: *Phaedr.* 235[a]	400 B.C.	22	*stupidity*
3	*Arist*: *Nic. Eth.* 1095a 25	350 B.C.		*ignorance*
4	Plato: *Symp.* 216[a].	400 B.C.	**21**, 22	*helplessness to resist Socrates when listening to him*
5	Arist: *Hist. An.* 618[a]. 26	350 B.C.	21	*cowardice* but see column X
6	Dem: *Ep.* II.20	(see Col. X)	**24**	*goodwill towards my country*
7	Soph: Fr. 669 (Dind.)	460 B.C.	**23**, 27, 43, 48	*being noble*
8	Xen: *Cyr.* I.v.11	410 B.C.	**23**, 24, 44, 97	*seek after righteousness*
9	Socrates (ap Stobaeus)*	430 B.C.	34, 47, **56**,	*untoward*
10	Xen: *Cyr.* I.vi.4	410 B.C.	**25**, 27, 41, 44	*neglect of virtue*
11	Plato: *Rep.* 331[a]	400 B.C.	22, 27, 50	*unrighteous*
12	Isoc: *to Philip* 79	400 B.C.	47	*committing sin*
13	Isoc: *to Nicocles* 59 (ap Stobaeus)*	400 B.C.	27, 34	*bad*

*All references to

VI	VII	VIII	IX	X
POSITIVE OR NEGATIVE	TENSE OF PARTICIPLE	RESULT FOR SUBJECT, of αὐτῷ συνειδέναι	CLASSIFI- CATION	REMARKS
Neg.	Pres.	—	PTI	—
—	—	—	PTI	—
—	—	*Follow opinions of others*	PTI	—
—	(Pres.)	—	PTI	The only case in which the content of αὐτῷ συνειδέναι is defined by an *oratio obliqua* clause–introduced by ὅτι.
—	—	*The cuckoo–abandons its young*	PTI	Here 'I know cowardice in myself' is defined as meaning 'I know myself unable to help'.
—	—	—	MPG	Epistle spuriously attributed to Demosthenes.
—	Pres.	*a powerful aid* (Jebb)	MPG	See Ex 35 below.
—	Aor. + pres. = perf.	—	MPG	—
Neg.	—	*trouble-free life*	MBNeg	—
Neg.	Aor.	*Joy in prayer and certainty of response*	MBNeg	—
Neg.	—	*a sweet hope, a good comfort in old age*	MBNeg	—
Neg.	Pres.	*If neg. removed–then by implication in preceding clause: meanness of spirit*	MBNeg	Norlin in Loeb edition renders: 'when your conscience is free from any sense of guilt.'
Neg.	—	*lead all his life most pleasantly*	MBNeg	Norlin, *ed.* Loeb avoids *conscience* here: but has to use it for ψυχή in second half of sentence.

A. *The Verbal Phrase*

αὐτῷ συνειδέναι

I	II	III	IV	V
SERIAL No.	REFERENCE TO SOURCE	APPROX. DATE FL.	REF. TO PAGE	CONTENT OF αὐτῷ συν εἰδέναι—I.E. PARTICIPLE ABSTRACT NOUN OR EQUIV
14	Antiphanes ap Stobaeus*	380 B.C.	27, 51	*a wrong*
15	Diogenes ap Stobaeus*	370 B.C.	27, 112	*bad*
16	*Syll* 567.7	ii A.D.	47, 50	*terrible*
17	Euripides: *Or.* 395 f	440 B.C.	26, 27, 30, 41, 44, 46, **47**, 49, 74, 82, 89, 112	*having done terrible things*
18	Euripides: *Med.* 495	440 B.C.	**26**, 33, 46	*you have not kept faith with me*
19	Aristophanes: *Wasps* 999	420 B.C.	25, 45	*acquitted a defendant*
20	Aristophanes: *Thesm.* 477	420 B.C.	46	*many terrible things (sexual corruption)*
21	Xen: *Anab.* II.v.7	410 B.C.	**24**, 25, 41, 44, 48, 112	*neglect of sacred oath*
22	Xen: *Mem.* II.ix.6	410 B.C.		*many wicked things*
23	Xen: *Apol.* 24	410 B.C.	**40**, 48, 50	*great sacrilege and unright eousness*
24	Xen: *Anab.* I.iii.10	410 B.C.	**112**	*utter deception of him*
25	Plato: *Rep.* 607ᵒ	400 B.C.	**22**	*bewitched–seduced*

VI	VII	VIII	IX	X
POSITIVE OR NEGATIVE	TENSE OF PARTICIPLE	RESULT FOR SUBJECT, of αὐτῷ συνειδέναι	CLASSIFICATION	REMARKS
Neg.	—	*great joy*	MBNeg	—
Neg.	—	*Freedom from fear, and great confidence*	MBNeg	—
Neg.	—	*Sweet innocence*	MBNeg	—
—	Perf.	*suffers from a disease which destroys*	MBNorm	Liddell and Scott comment: σύνεσις = συνείδησις· = Ex 56 q.v.
—	Pres.	—	MBNorm	N.B. in both Euripides' examples prosody compels the omission of the reflexive pronoun: also Negative οὐ when litotes intended.
—	Aor.	*Distress: fear*–prayer for pardon to the Gods.	MBNorm	Cf. *ibid*. 160. N.B. hint in τοῦτο of abs. use of phrase. Cf. example 33 below.
—	Aor. (implied in previous sentence: δρώσας)	NIL–but see Col. X.	MBNorm	Speaker a fraud: her claim σύνοιδα ἐμαυτῇ is false.
—	Perf.	One who does so *can never be called happy*	MBNorm	
—	—	desperation: *tried every way*	MBNorm	
—	—	[συνειδέναι αὐτῷ, by implication, punishment enough in itself]	MBNorm	N.B. Such suffering is of the order of 'Ανάγκη.
—	Perf.	Unwilling to go when summoned.	MBNorm	In comparison with fear of punishment, ὅτι σύνοιδα ἐμαυτῷ is τὸ μὲν μέγιστον.
—	Pres.	seductive thing to be expelled from ideal society	MBNorm	

A. *The Verbal Phrase*

αὐτῷ συνειδέναι

I	II	III	IV	V
SERIAL No.	REFERENCE TO SOURCE	APPROX. DATE FL.	REF. TO PAGE	CONTENT OF αὐτῷ συνειδέναι—I.E. PARTICIPLE, ABSTRACT NOUN OR EQUIV.
26	Plato: *Symp.* 216ᵇ	400 B.C.	22, 112	*cannot but choose the good in theory, under Socrates' guidance: but in practice abandons good intentions for lowest of motives*
27	Isoc: *to Demonicus* 16 (ap Stobaeus)*	400 B.C.	48, **74**	*shameful*
28	Dem: *de Fals. Leg.* 208	340 B.C.	24, 32, 40, **48**	*betrayal of public trust for a bribe*
29	Dem: *de Fals. Leg.* 210	340 B.C.	24	*receiving, or sharing, bribes: referred to by* ταῦτα
30	Dem: *de Corona* 263	340 B.C.	24, 30, **48**, 50, 112	*being unrighteous*
31	Diphilus ap Stobaeus*	320 B.C.	112	*having done base things*
32	*Pap. Oxy.* vi. 898²⁰	123 A.D.	46	*having plundered a great deal of another's property*
33	Arist.: *Knights* 184	420 B.C.	25, **45**, 109	καλόν τι
34	Menander: Fr. 632 (Kock) ap Stobaeus*	310 B.C.	18, **25**, 26, 30, 43, 48, 112	τι (κακόν taken for granted)
35	Stobaeus: III xxiv.6 (quoting Soph.)	v-vi A.D.	**23**, 27, 43, 48	*Abs. use:* κακόν τι *taken for granted*

VI	VII	VIII	IX	X
POSITIVE OR NEGATIVE	TENSE OF PARTICIPLE	RESULT FOR SUBJECT, of αὐτῷ συνειδέναι	CLASSIFI-CATION	REMARKS
—	Pres.	*I am ashamed: I have suffered*	MBNorm	
—	Aor.	such as is as much to be feared as result of discovery by others.	MBNorm	
—	Perf.	inferiority in face of truth, and its representatives although insignificant, *constricts, reduces to silence*, etc.	MBNorm	Dem., using the phrase twice in a single passage, uses τὸ συνειδέναι at the end as though it were τὸ συνειδός.
—	Perf.	*cowers like a slave*	MBNorm	
—	Pres.	*in fear and trembling, and always in the expectation of blows*	MBNorm	
—	Perf.	*shame the natural and proper reaction*	MBNorm	
—	Perf.	—	MBNorm	
—	—	*hesitation to pursue public office on part of rogue*	MBA	Sarcasm–depends for point on popular understanding from αὐτῷ συνειδέναι that καλόν here = κακόν.
—	—	extreme of *cowardice* even in the *boldest*	MBA	Koch comments: συνιστορῶν = συνειδώς· = Ex 57 *q.v.*
—	—	*a terrible thing for anyone who is noble*	MBA	Cf. No. 7 above: see p. 23, n. 6*a* for reason for repetition. N.B. overtones of Ἀνάγκη, cf. p. 40, n. 4.

B. *The Substantives*

(i) τὸ συνειδός

I	II	III	IV	V
SERIAL No.	REFERENCE TO SOURCE	APPROX. DATE FL.	REF. TO PAGE	EPITHET AND/OR REFERENCE
36	Dem: *de Corona* 110	340 B.C.	**30**, 88	knowledge shared *with each one of* [his hearers]
37	Pausanias VII.x.10	180 A.D.	**37**	ἀγαθόν
38	Alciphron I.x.5	200 A.D.	35, 43, 106	*beneficence: good works*
39	*Pap. Reinach* lii.5	iii-iv A.D.	**37**, 43, 47	καλόν
40	Heliodorus vi.7	390 A.D.	**35**, 43	ἀγαθόν–duty of guardian worthily performed
41	Stobaeus III.xxiv	v-vi A.D.	**16**, 30, 35, 46	
42	Josephus: *Bell. Jud.* I.xxiii.3	70 A.D.	**37**	καθαρόν
43	*Orphic Hymn* LXIII 3 f	? A.D.	37, **49**	*Justice* by implication *has no wrong doing* on her conscience
44	*Pap. Oxy.* III 532[23]	ii A.D.	**58**	κακόν
45	Pythagoras (?) ap Stobaeus*	(536 B.C.)		*the unrighteous man* is subj.
46	Philo: Fr. ed. Mang. II, p. 652	40 A.D.	41, **49**	absolute

VI	VII	VIII	IX
SIMILE OR OTHER DESCRIPTION	RESULT FOR SUBJECT	CLASSIFICATION	REMARKS
—	D. can afford to omit ref. to policy and administration	NA	$= \sigma \upsilon \nu \epsilon \iota \delta \acute{\epsilon} \nu \alpha \iota$ and NOT $\alpha \mathring{\upsilon} \tau \mathring{\omega} \ \sigma.$ which D. uses when he means that, cf. Exx 28 to 30 above.
	frankness of speaker	MPG (?)	Borderline case–see n. 4 *ad loc.*
—	*delight* no less than afforded by material *reward*	MPG	
—	lack of $\tau \grave{o} \ \kappa \alpha \lambda \acute{o} \nu \ \sigma.$ leads to to neglect	MPG (?)	Negative deceptive–see n. 4 *ad loc.*
—	$\mathring{\alpha} \gamma \alpha \theta \acute{o} \nu \ \sigma.$ itself sufficient reward	MPG	
—	—	MB (A?)	Chapter heading only.
—	[ability as a speaker]	MBNeg	
—	Justice is *unbroken as to conscience*	MBNeg	*Conscience*, also by implication, the means whereby Justice *breaks* the *wrong-doers*.
—	*constraint*	MBNorm	
—	suffers worse than if flogged	MBA	Perhaps 'Pythagorean' rather than 'by Pythagoras'.
—	*self-condemnation*	MBA	See remarks below on Exx 47 f which apply to Philo in general.

B. *The Substantives*
   (i) τὸ συνειδός

SERIAL No.	REFERENCE TO SOURCE	APPROX. DATE FL.	REF. TO PAGE	EPITHET AND/OR REFERENCE
47	Philo: *QDSI* 128	40 A.D.	31, 41, 46, **49**, 51, 58, 96	
48	Philo: *QDPIS* 23	40 A.D.	31, **41**, 46, **58**	*curb of conscience*
49	Plutarch: *de Tranquillitate Animi* 476ᶠ-477ᴬ	80 A.D.	31, **47** f, 49, 58, 82, 89, 91	—
50	Plutarch: *Quomodo quis suos in virtute sentiat profectus* 84ᴰ	80 A.D.	31, 49, 106, **127**	*of his falling short* (by comparison with the works of the *good and perfect man*)
51	Plutarch: *De sera numinis vindicta* 556ᴬ	80 A.D.	31, **34** f, 48, 115	—
52	Plutarch: *Publicola* iv.99ᴮ	80 A.D.	31, 43, 49, 106, **115**	*of the affair*
53	Dio Chrysostom: *Corinthiaca* 35	100 A.D.	49	—
54	Epictetus: Fr. 97 (Schweighaüser)	90? A.D.	13, 15, 31, 41, 49, **51** f, 58, 74, **124**	*our own*
55	*OGIS* 484.37	ii A.D.	49, **50**	—

(ii) ἡ σύνεσις

SERIAL No.	REFERENCE TO SOURCE	APPROX. DATE FL.	REF. TO PAGE	EPITHET AND/OR REFERENCE
56	Euripides: *Orestes* 395 f	440 B.C.	26, 27, 30, 41, 44, 46, **47**, 49, 74, 82, 89, 112	*having done terrible things*

VI	VII	VIII	IX
SIMILE OR OTHER DESCRIPTION	RESULT FOR SUBJECT	CLASSIFI- CATION	REMARKS
terrible accuser: judge	*rebuked*	MBA	In Philo τὸ σ. resides in nature of man as man. Cf. de Decalogo 87 (cited p. 47) on ὁ ἔλεγχος and note.
witness: accuser	*[rebukes from within]: bridles*	MBA	
ulcer in the flesh: pain: suffering	*chastened from within*	MBA	Hung on peg of quotation from Euripides: *Or.* 395 f, Exx 17 and 56.
—	*gnawed*	MBA	
parallel with *the memory of its ill-deeds*	must be *cast out* before a new start in life can be made and the soul become pure	MBA	
—	*impelled*	MBA	*the affair* is another's projected deed: τὸ συνειδός here refers to silence about it which equals consent.
—	*frankness* forced on him by fear of τὸ σ. more than of the judge	MBA	Cf. Ex 37 above.
None–but cf. on συνείδησις in same context and passage, Ex 84 below	to be *at enmity with* τὸ σ. is to be thereby *ill-pleasing to God*	MBA	Wrongly attributed to Epictetus: see pp. 13, 15 and nn. Explicit reference to God in relation to τὸ συνειδός. = Ex 84
—	unable to swear because of, or by τὸ σ.	MBA	διά might just possibly indicate the thing sworn by. But it should almost certainly be taken here to mean *because of*.
a disease	he *suffers* from it: it *destroys* him	MBNorm	Recurrence of Ex 17, *q.v.*

B. *The Substantives*

(ii) ἡ σύνεσις

I	II	III	IV	V
SERIAL No.	REFERENCE TO SOURCE	APPROX. DATE FL.	REF. TO PAGE	EPITHET AND/OR REFERENCE
57	Menander: Fr. (Kock) 632	310 B.C.	18, **25**, 26, 30, 43, 48, 112	τι
58	Polybius XVIII.xliii.13	170 B.C.	31, **41**	—
59	Herodian IV.vii.1	240 A.D.	43, 49, 58, **106**, 115	*what was done*

(iii) ἡ συνείδησις

60	Soranus i.4	ii A.D.	**30**	*of the pains* of childbirth (in another)
61	Hippocrates: *Ep.* I	430 B.C.	30	ἀγαθῇ
62	*Pap. Par.* p. 422.7	ii A.D.	30	—
63	*Pap. Oxy.* I.123.13	iii-iv A.D.	30	—
64	Herodian: *Hist.* vii.1.3	240 A.D.		*noble*
65	Chrysippus ap Diog. Laert. vii.85	240 B.C.	**14**, 22, 29	*of its own constitution*
66	Menander: *Monost.* 654	310 B.C.	**41**, 46, 111, 122	—
67	Periander ap Stobaeus*	vi B.C.	**37**	ἀγαθή
68	Bias ap Stobaeus*	vi B.C.	**37**, 112	ὀρθή

VI	VII	VIII	IX
SIMILE OR OTHER DESCRIPTION	RESULT FOR SUBJECT	CLASSIFICATION	REMARKS
—	*it makes him an utter coward though he be bravest of men*	MBA	Recurrence of Ex 34, *q.v.*
fearful witness: terrible accuser		MBA	Cf. Exx 46-48 (Philo)–same simile used with notion of *dwelling in every soul.*
—	so *impelled* as to desire to quit Rome	MBA	Cf. Ex. 52. Herodian also employs συνείδησις: see Ex 69.
—	she who has such σ. makes the best midwife	NA	Complementary to *suffering with.*
—	—	NA	*heureux avis*–(medical).
—	—	NA	*les gens au courant.*
—	—	NA	εἰσφέρειν συνείδησιν = *certiorem facere.*
—	—	NA	Obscure sense: might be taken as *character*–but context seems to require *birth –extraction–descent.*
the most 'personal' thing for every living creature	—	PTI	*consciousness.*
Divine for all mortals	—	M	—
—	*liberty*	MPG ?	Doubtful classifications–insufficient data–and, if MPG, these only cases of such: oral tradition in any case.
—	*life free from fear*	MPG ?	

B. *The Substantives*

(iii) ἡ συνείδησις

I	II	III	IV	V
SERIAL No.	REFERENCE TO SOURCE	APPROX. DATE FL.	REF. TO PAGE	EPITHET AND/OR REFERENCE
69	Herodian: *Hist.* VI.iii.4	240 A.D.	27, **36** ff	ἀγαθή = *without doing wrong*
70	*Arch. Pap.* iii.418.13	vi A.D.	37, **126**	*unwavering*
71	*Pap. Par.* 21.15	616 A.D.	37, **126**	*guileless*
72	Democritus: Fr. 297 (Diels)	430 B.C.	17, 22, **34**, 41, 49, 106, 112,	*of the evil-doing in their lives*
73	*Test XII Patr: Reub.* iv.3	135-103 B.C.	49, 58	*concerning the sin*
74	Philodemus: *Rhet.* ii.140	50 B.C.	106	*of such a life*, i.e. one of *litigiousness*
75	Dion. Halicarn: *de Thuc. jud.* viii.3	30 B.C.	**50**, 81, 92	*deliberately to falsify facts*
76	Dion. Halicarn: *Ant.* viii.1.3	30 B.C.	**31** f, 49	*having dealt with them terribly (in war)*
77	Dion. Halicarn: *Ant.* viii.48.5	30 B.C.	106	*unjust and sacrilegious*
78	Diodorus Siculus iv.65	10 B.C.	41, 49, **74**, 106	*of the abominable act* [i.e. matricide]
79	Philo: Fr. ed. Mang. II, p. 659	40 A.D.	41, **48**, 49, 106, 112	*of a base act*, or possibly, *base man*
80	Lucian: *Amores* 49	160 A.D.	106	*of unseemliness*

VI	VII	VIII	IX
SIMILE OR OTHER DESCRIPTION	RESULT FOR SUBJECT	CLASSIFI-CATION	REMARKS
—	*great confidence . . . cheerful hope*	MBNeg	Result arises from combination of such σ. with *shaking one's self free of those who are troubling one*, and *defending* (or, *avenging*) *one's self.*
—	statement validated	MBNeg	N.B. Contrast of σ. with προαίρεσις. Apparently conventional or perhaps legal formulae for Solemn Declaration.
—	statement validated	MBNeg	
—	*suffer wretchedly from distress and fear, etc.*	MBNorm	*The ignorant mass of mankind* so suffer.
—	*constrains me*	MBNorm	—
—	*meet with ruin*	MBNorm	Classification thus probable only.
—	*stains the σ.* of the historian	MBNorm	Sadaeus regards as *adnotationem lectoris Christiani*-but reasons not clear: no MS. evidence.
—	*troubled him*	MBNorm	—
—	(protest that boon craved is pure of such σ.)	MBNorm	Unusual construction–transference of συνείδησις from pleader to plea.
σ. here substituted for Eumenides of original legend	*went completely mad*	MBNorm	Cf. Euripides on Orestes Legend, *Or.* 395 f: Exx 17 and 56.
as from a blow	*sufficient punishment . . . inducing great fear in the soul*	MBNorm	Interpretation the same whether τοῦ φαύλου masc. or neut.
—	*The time of life is most sweet* in the absence of such σ.	MBNorm	—

B. *The Substantives*

(iii) ἡ συνείδησις

I SERIAL No.	II REFERENCE TO SOURCE	III APPROX. DATE FL.	IV REF. TO PAGE	V EPITHET AND/OR REFERENCE
81	*Supp. Epigr.* IV.648.13	ii A.D.	42, **48**	inducing madness in son-in-law by poisoning
82	*Pap. Oxy.* II.218ª. ii.19	iii A.D.	41, 106	*of any crime*
83	Hero: [*Vet. Mech. Op.* (Paris 1693) p. 122.2]	250 B.C.	50	—
84	Epictetus: Fr. 97 (Schweighaüser)	90? A.D.	13, 15, 31, 41, 49, **51** f, 58, 74, 124	—
85	Vettius Valens V.i	ii A.D.	40, 41, 49, 50, **58**, 74	—
86	*Pap. Ryl.* II.116.9	194 A.D.	43, 49	*about the things she had purloined*
87	*Pap. Flor.* 338.17	iii A.D.		—
88	*Pap. BGU,* IV. 1024.iii.7	iv A.D.	43, **48**, 106, 126	*of what has been done*
89	*Ath. Mitt.* xxiv.237	v A.D.	42, 43, **72**	(interference with or desecration of tombstone)

VI	VII	VIII	IX
SIMILE OR OTHER DESCRIPTION	RESULT FOR SUBJECT	CLASSIFI-CATION	REMARKS
—	*a chastisement from which she did not escape*	MBNorm	from Lydia. N.B. *The Gods did this.*
—	trial by ordeal reveals it–culprit must answer to Ares	MBNorm	Trials by ordeal, etc., pre-suppose relationship–be-tween σ. and behaviour of physical matter.
—	*undisturbed* if take pains about armament	MBA	—
nursery-slave	*Both displeasing to God, and at enmity with our own σ.*	MBA	Wrongly attributed to Epic-tetus. σ. is *implanted*. N.B. double reference to God in relation to σ. See also Ex 54.
obstacle like islands to the seafarer or deserts to the traveller	*constrained; restrained; chastised* or *held in check*	MBA	Contrast between external and internal pressure. Re-striction to a particular horoscope apparent only.
—	a: *oppressed,* so b: resorts to violence	MBA	—
—	*is zealous*	MBA	Casual use of dat.: equivalent to our *conscientiously.*
VI	the leader is warned to *walk in fear of σ.*	MBA	Occurrence of προαίρεσις as distinct and complement-ary, cf. Ex 70. But text very defective.
—	(a) *God angered* (b) *His own σ.* (c) Civil penalties	MBA	This date and presumption of Christian influence and origin (cf. Rom. 12-14) deduced from internal evidence. See text *ad loc.,* and n.

INDEX OF BIBLICAL REFERENCES

OLD TESTAMENT